C000077655

THE A-Z OF CURIOUS

COUNTY DURHAM

MARTIN DUFFERWIEL

The History Press

First published 2014

The History Press
The Mill, Brimscombe Port
Stroud, Gloucestershire, GL5 2QG
www.thehistorypress.co.uk

© Martin Dufferwiel, 2014

The right of Martin Dufferwiel to be identified as the Author
of this work has been asserted in accordance with the
Copyright, Designs and Patents Act 1988.

All rights reserved. No part of this book may be reprinted
or reproduced or utilised in any form or by any electronic,
mechanical or other means, now known or hereafter invented,
including photocopying and recording, or in any information
storage or retrieval system, without the permission in writing
from the Publishers.

British Library Cataloguing in Publication Data.
A catalogue record for this book is available from the British Library.

ISBN 978 0 7524 9314 5

Typesetting and origination by The History Press
Printed in Great Britain

Contents

Acknowledgements   4

Introduction   5

The A–Z of Curious County Durham   7

Afterword   158

Bibliography   159

Acknowledgements

First of all, my thanks go to my family, for their patience and support during the preparation of this book.

Thanks also go to Helen Thompson, Divisional Librarian, and to the Durham County Library Service, for permission to reproduce illustrations from the titles listed under Standard References in the Bibliography, all of which can be viewed at Durham Clayport Library. As always I am grateful to staff of the Reference Section of the library for their knowledge and courtesy, and especially to Anita Thompson for her unfailingly polite assistance and ever-useful advice.

I am indebted to Mr Philip Davies, Chapter Clerk, Durham Cathedral, for his kind assistance. The photographs of St Cuthbert's feretory are reproduced by kind permission of the Chapter of Durham.

I would also like to express my gratitude to Kate van Suddese, for kindly allowing me sight of her grandfather's collected but unpublished notes concerning the history of his beloved Durham City, some of which I have been happy to reproduce in this book.

Introduction

Has nothing been, because the sound if it has died away from dull ears?

Sir Timothy Eden

This book is inspired in part by the wonderful and extensive chronicles, journals and periodicals committed to print by the historians, antiquarians and other seekers after the odd and the curious in Georgian and Victorian County Durham.

An anthology of fact, anecdote and collected folklore, it is also a miscellany of notable individuals, surprising events and strange happenings throughout the historical County Palatine, bounded by the River Tyne in the north and the River Tees in the south. Though written in an 'A–Z' format, the interpretation of that format and the narrative is left quite loose, to reflect the style of the old chronicles upon which it is based.

A small number of subjects have been covered in more detail in my previous books and apologies to all if this seems like repetition, but they remain curious, and as such have a rightful place in this particular book. There are also simple anecdotes of which, though perhaps slightly odd, some readers may think that the only truly *curious* thing about them is why they have been included at all. But they at least caught the eye of the author and were thought to have merit enough to be passed on.

And so, in the following pages, the reader will find stories of murder and mystery, visions and vanishings, as well as a sample of the many ghosts that lurk in Durham's shadows.

Samuel Johnson, writing in the eighteenth century, said of the appearance of ghosts: 'All argument is against it; but all belief is for it.' For the modern reader it may appear that little has changed. Certainly we all enjoy a good ghost story whether we believe it to be entirely genuine, a hoax perpetrated upon the credulous, or a complete fabrication of events intended to achieve a specific response or result. A good haunting can also mean good marketing! Some ghost accounts related today as being genuine do seem to be supported by being set in a credible, if sometimes vague, historical context. Strangely, however, little or no account of them can be found in older chronicles, where perhaps it would be expected that they should be recorded.

But this is not meant to be a book about the ghosts of County Durham and there are a number of excellent publications on that particular subject, by authors far more expert on it than this one.

Of course many old stories, whether ghostly or not, will have undergone numerous developments over the years; variations, embellishments or perhaps even just being tweaked to make them more relevant or believable to a new or a different audience. And the curious can often search in vain for the definitive version. Indeed there have been in the past those gentleman antiquarians (the great historian of County Durham Robert Surtees among them) who had an easy and regular skill in discovering new old tales. Perhaps they really did come from the historical record, or perhaps from an indistinct and elusive source; perhaps occasionally from a certain old woman known only to the author, or from the grandfather of an anonymous servant; or perhaps, directly from their own imagination.

In this book, the reader will come across some tales – both ancient and recent – that are already well known and some characters that are familiar to us today as having played a significant role in the long story of County Durham. But the majority of the subjects are, quite literally, footnotes from our county's history. Perhaps this book will bring their story to a new readership. For in the words of James Clepham, first written down in 1888 and recorded for posterity in the second volume of the *Monthly Chronicle*:

> The myths and marvels of the morning time, the good old stories and legends, the tales of our grandfathers and of theirs, shall forever be a human heritage.

Martin Dufferwiel,
2014

✤ ALFRED'S VISION ✤

Among the pictures exhibited at the Royal Academy in 1890 was a painting entitled *The Sanctuary* by the Newcastle artist Ralph Hedley. It is an imagined depiction of 'what may have been a not unusual scene at the Great Door of Durham Cathedral, centuries ago'.

In AD 871, Alfred of Wessex defeated the invading Danes at the Battle of Ashdown in Berkshire. Soon after, however, his fortunes were reversed and by the middle of the same decade he was in hiding, deep in the Somerset marshes. His army defeated, his people scattered and faced by the all-conquering Great Heathen Army of Danish Vikings, he despaired for his own fate and for the fate of his kingdom. Hundreds of miles away, off the Northumberland coast, the same Viking threat had forced the monks of Lindisfarne to leave their beloved island home. Taking with them the body of St Cuthbert and their sacred gospels and relics, they began a long journey, seeking refuge in safe places; a journey that would lead eventually to Durham.

The story tells that one night, in his darkest despair, Alfred was approached by a beggar who asked him for food. Without question, Alfred gave half of the meagre provisions that he had, but the mysterious beggar simply disappeared into the night, leaving the food untouched. That same night Alfred had a vision of an aged priest holding a copy of the Gospels, adorned with gold and precious stones, saying 'I am he to whom you gave your charity. I am Cuthbert, the soldier of Christ; be strong, and without fear, for God has given your enemy into your hands.' So it was that in AD 878, Alfred prevailed over his enemy and became known to history as King Alfred the Great, the only English king ever to be given that epithet.

Alfred never forgot his vision of St Cuthbert and the strength that it had given him; he decreed that henceforward 'St Cuthbert's church should be a safe sanctuary for all fugitives'.

After their initial wanderings, the Community of St Cuthbert eventually made their way back to the North East. Here they were granted, 'freed of all customs and services forever', extensive lands between the rivers Wear and Tyne by the Danish chief, Guthred. Shortly afterwards their abbot had a dream in which, so he related, St Cuthbert had instructed him to go to Guthred and: 'Command him, moreover, to make my church a sure refuge for fugitives, that everyone, for whatever reason he may flee to my body, may enjoy inviolable protection.' Needless to say that this command, which had been confirmed by King Alfred, was obeyed by Guthred.

Indeed, the right of sanctuary would continue to be held inviolate by Alfred's Anglo-Saxon successors,

'The Sanctuary', a line drawing from a painting by Ralph Hedley.

by later Norman conquerors and by medieval kings. And so it was that Durham Cathedral, the eventual permanent resting place of St Cuthbert's body, with its almost mystical power as the guardian of his shrine, would remain (until Tudor times) one of the main places of refuge in the whole of northern England.

Around the year 1140, the sanctuary knocker, familiar to visitors today, was hung on the great North Door of the cathedral. A representation of 'some monstrous beast, unknown, save in the literature and art of fabledom', the bronze lion-like head with its strange, tendril-like mane protruding behind, became, literally, the face of sanctuary at Durham Cathedral; and the image that every fugitive, whether fleeing from oppression, justice or revenge, sought out.

Every church offered a basic right of sanctuary to a criminal. However, sites acknowledged by a king as being of special significance offered a higher degree of sanctuary, including protection from treasonable offences. Such sites might be connected with the shrine of a saint, such as Durham Cathedral, or with a site of martyrdom and consequently had a higher religious, and therefore symbolic, authority. Indeed, one Robert Marshall claimed sanctuary at Durham Cathedral for the offence of high treason against the king, thought to be either Henry IV or Henry V, and the king himself acknowledged the sanctity of Marshall's protection at Durham.

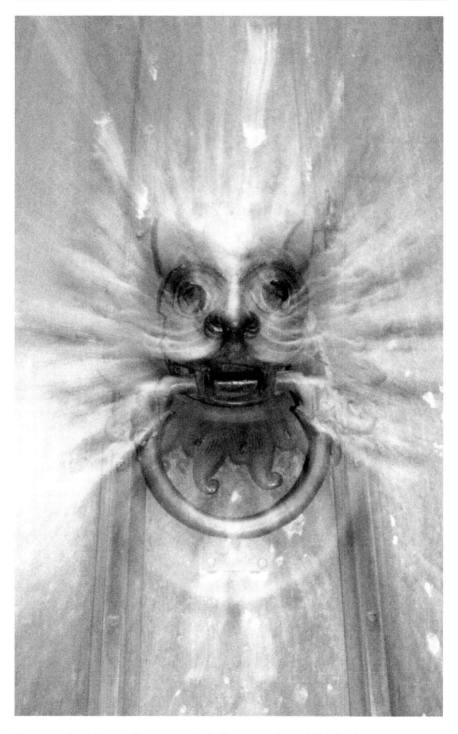

'Some monstrous beast, unknown, save in the literature and art of fabledom.'

The sanctuary knocker.   The great North Door of Durham Cathedral today.

Over the years, however, the protection of the Church came to be abused by canny criminals keen to use it simply to avoid trial by a jury, or to escape the wrath of their victims. Eventually, in Tudor times, a lawbreaker's sanctuary rights began to be reduced and their significance eroded. All treasonable offences were removed from the protection of the Church and eventually, in the year 1624, King James I passed an Act to abolish the right of sanctuary, ending this sacred and historic right with the rather prosaic words: 'Be it also enacted, that no Sanctuary or privilege of Sanctuary shall hereafter be allowed in any case.'

At Durham, before the year 1464, there is no written record to tell us who and how many claimed the sanctuary of St Cuthbert's church, or the nature of the offences that had brought them there. But it is to be imagined that the desperate hands of many had clasped the smooth bronze handle that hangs from the lion's mouth and hammered out their claim. The records kept from 1464 onwards tell us that between that year and the year 1524, 331 souls claimed sanctuary at Durham Cathedral. Of those, 195 were murderers, but their number also included horse thieves, cattle rustlers and burglars and they came from as far afield as Lincolnshire, Northamptonshire and Derbyshire.

The hollow hammering of Durham's sanctuary knocker was last heard on 10 September 1524, at that place 'where all those religious and mystic influences, had, for ages, gathered around the incorruptible body of one who was regarded as amongst the greatest Saints in Christendom'. And which (because of Alfred's vision deep in the Somerset marshes some six and a half centuries before) had become over those centuries, 'one of the most celebrated Sanctuaries in England'.

⚜ APPETITES ⚜

These days we are constantly being told, or so it seems, to watch our diet. Too much of any one thing and indeed general overindulgence in food or alcohol is, as we are relentlessly reminded, bad for us. However, at the same time, we are assured that everything is fine in moderation and just make sure that you get your 'five a day'.

For Mark Shafto of Whitworth, five a day would fall somewhat short of the norm. An ancestor of Bonny Bobby Shafto, Mark had an epithet of his own, for he was known the county round as Six Bottle Mark. This, we are told by J.J. Dodd in his *History of the Urban District of Spennymoor*, refers to his general fondness for imbibing and in particular to the amount of port wine he would consume at any one sitting.

Dodd tells us that an inscription on the wall of Whitworth church extols Mark Shafto's virtues of being amiable, liberal, pious, and humble and a source of great hilarity amongst his peers. It finishes with the subtle but knowing allusion to his epithet, proclaiming him 'easier to be praised than imitated'.

Reverend John Tyson of Kirk Merrington likewise had a fondness for the bottle. Faced with a less than enthusiastic congregation, Tyson, we are told, kept a supply of whisky in the vestry which he used to 'fortify him for the pulpit'. And it was from the vestry that one day, before service, Tyson processed into the church in great solemnity, with head bowed and his eyes closed in spiritual contemplation. On reaching the pulpit and beginning with the words 'Dearly beloved brethren', he looked up and saw that his congregation consisted solely of the verger. With a sigh of resignation, Tyson snapped shut his Bible and invited the verger back to the vestry for a drink.

Tyson, we are told, was also a stickler for the collection of his tithes. An ancient duty, the collection of tithes was particularly unpopular with farmers, who had to provide the Church with a tenth of everything they produced. A local farmer once thought he'd escaped the scrutiny of Revd Tyson, ever vigilant for what was due to him. The good reverend, it seemed, had missed a brood of ten goslings the farmer had reared. However, one day, when the geese were grown and fat, the vicar's agent seized one of them as they were leaving the farmyard. On asking Tyson why he hadn't taken the bird when it was little, the farmer was told, 'I waited till it was ready'.

Indeed, Tyson's fondness for the bottle seems to have been more than matched by his fondness for food; lots of it, and regularly. He was well known for his prodigious appetite and was once heard to declare that a whole goose 'was too much for one, but too little for two'. He also enjoyed mutton, of which he would happily consume a whole leg at his dinner. Tyson was a nightmare for local innkeepers – often, during his visits, he would consume provisions intended for other guests whilst being distinctly parsimonious with his payment.

Kirk Merrington church.

Revd John Tyson: 'The innkeepers of Durham dreaded his coming.'

Gowland's inn was situated in New Elvet, Durham and, during his frequent visits to St Cuthbert's city, was a favourite haunt of Revd Tyson. Consequently, Gowland knew him very well and had even been heard berating the hungry Tyson when he'd arrived at his door: 'Now Tyson, a canna de with ye for eighteen pence, a canna de with ye!' So Gowland knew what to expect when one day Tyson returned and, on entering, left in the hallway of the inn a leg of mutton that he had just purchased for his own private home consumption. Seeing his opportunity, Gowland instructed his man to take the mutton to the kitchen and have it prepared for the vicar's repast. This was done and, to the relief of Mr Gowland, the continued healthiness of his store of provisions, and to the satisfaction of Revd Tyson's hunger, the leg was duly consumed.

What Tyson's reaction was when he discovered that he had devoured his own leg of mutton is not recorded, but at least Gowland did not charge him for his meal!

⁕ BRIDEWELL'S GUEST ⁕

It was the summer of the year 1799. The last twelve months had been good for Mary Nicholson, considering her situation.

Those twelve months had seen Mary living in Durham City and dutifully attending to her chores and to the wishes of her master and his family. Going about her business in the city, she had become acquainted and had made friends with many of the townspeople. She had become a familiar face and was universally liked. But Mary Nicholson's year was almost over.

Mary, moreover, was no ordinary servant girl; her current master was the gaoler of the house of correction: the Bridewell. The second of the city's prisons, it was almost buried beneath Elvet Bridge and, since 1634, had been a filthy, rat-infested home to murderers, thieves, vagrants, debtors, drunks and those awaiting trial or execution. And it was a notorious incident indeed that had led Mary to be resident at such a grim and undesirable address.

Elvet Bridge. The Bridewell was behind the steps on the right of the bridge.

Mary Nicholson was a quiet young woman, an orphan, and for a number of years she had worked as a servant girl in the outwardly respectable household of farmer John Atkinson of Little Stainton. But Mary had a childlike intellect, her mental age fell well short of her years and there had been dark and uncomfortable rumours that Atkinson 'had taken great liberties and behaved very cruelly to her'. The truth behind these rumours seems to have been borne out for, by April 1798, Mary could take no more from John Atkinson and decided to have her revenge. Whilst shopping in Darlington she procured some arsenic powder, then commonly available from any general dealers. She claimed it was needed for washing sheep.

Mary returned to the household and proceeded to mix the arsenic powder with flour so that she could make John Atkinson one of his favourite puddings. But that day, her plan, such as it was, went wrong. Her master was not hungry and the deadly flour mixture was left unused. Seeing the flour mixture, however, the matriarch of the household (John Atkinson's mother, Elizabeth Atkinson) took it and made a loaf of bread, which the whole family then shared. All five members of the household became violently ill. A doctor was sent for and four of them were brought back from the brink. The fifth, Elizabeth Atkinson herself, lingered in agony for sixteen days before eventually dying.

Mary Nicholson was distraught. Horrified at what had happened, she freely admitted to three different people that the responsibility for the tragedy was hers. She further confessed to planning to poison John Atkinson in revenge for certain 'bad deeds' he had inflicted upon her. The modern reader can only guess at the enormities which Mary may have been subjected to by her master. Bizarrely, however, the Atkinson family simply dismissed her from their service, telling her that if she left and never returned to their house they would take no proceedings against her. But Mary had nobody to turn to and she had nowhere to go. For some time she wandered the countryside, aimless, homeless, wretched and starving. Although occasionally taken in and fed by farmers such as a Mr Ord in Newfield, the poor girl could see no future for herself and returned to the Atkinson household to appeal for their mercy. She was promptly handed over to the authorities.

Mary was sent for trial in Durham City at the Summer Assizes of 1798. Heard before Mr Justice le Blanc, her case, so it seemed to the court, was an open and shut one and the verdict was duly returned, proclaiming her guilty of wilful murder. Mary was sentenced to death.

But there was a problem. She had been charged and indicted for intentionally conniving to murder Elizabeth Atkinson, which clearly was not true. She had freely admitted her desire to end the life of John Atkinson, using the poisoned flour, but in the end she hadn't done it. She had done nothing with the poisoned flour. She hadn't even prepared the fatal loaf of bread; Elizabeth Atkinson had done that, dooming herself. The death of Elizabeth Atkinson had not been brought about intentionally, or in a premeditated fashion, by Mary Nicholson and there was a strong argument to say, therefore, that the death was not murder. A skilful lawyer could even perhaps have claimed that it had been a tragic accident.

A prosecution could fail if a fault in the actual indictment could be proven. Mary Nicholson, however, was alone in court. She had nobody to speak for her and no legal representative to press home the argument. Nonetheless, a point of law was raised regarding the indictment and, by implication, the sentence. The issue would be passed to a higher authority and Mary was given a temporary reprieve. Details of her case were sent to the twelve judges sitting at the Common Law Courts in Westminster and in the event it would take another year before Mary knew her ultimate fate. For the immediate future, Mary would be remanded in custody in Durham City, in the dreaded Bridewell.

From the outset of that year, Mary began doing what she knew best: an honest job. She gained the trust of the gaoler, eventually working as an unofficial housekeeper for his family. So hardworking, reliable and diligent was she, that she was eventually fully accepted into their domestic circle, winning their sympathy. She was indeed proving to be an exemplary individual and over the following months she was freely allowed to go on errands around the city. By all accounts she grew to be on friendly terms with many of the shopkeepers and tradesmen with whom she had the day-to-day dealings of a housekeeper, eventually becoming a well-known and well-liked face in Durham City. In time all restrictions on her movements were lifted but, despite the terrible shadow which hung over her, and though she oft times had the opportunity to do so, never once over those twelve months did Mary attempt to escape. She never did display the actions of a murderess awaiting execution.

And so the year passed and the month of July returned. The Durham Assize sat in session and the day of Mary's judgement arrived. The whole bad business would surely now be brought to an end. Mary's was the first case to be heard and, in view of her year-long incarceration, the presiding judge was quick to hand down the final decision of the justices of the Common Law Courts: Mary Nicholson was to be hanged the following Saturday, 22 July 1799.

People in the courtroom were horrified. Surely, they thought, this could not be right. Surely the same girl that had become so familiar to so many people in Durham City over the last year could not be some cold-hearted murderess, justly doomed to the gallows. But the decision had been made. The execution was to take place, so the chronicles record, on Framwellgate Moor.

Mary Nicholson's final few days went by and the day of her execution soon dawned. A large crowd gathered on the moor to show their respects to the friend they had made and to give to her what support they could during her final ordeal. Mary was taken to the gallows on the back of a cart and when she got there, bearing herself with dignity, said sad farewells to those whom she had come to know well over the past year. When the time came and all holy rites had been done, the horse was clipped, the cart rolled away and as the rope tightened, Mary Nicholson glimpsed eternity.

But as she swung, the rope which was slowly ending her life suddenly snapped and Mary fell to the ground in a swoon. To the assembled crowd it seemed that at last, perhaps through divine intervention, real justice had been granted to Mary; she had been reprieved for a second time and this time seemingly by a much higher power than mere earthly judges. She was quickly revived by friends. Her fate was of course still in the hands of the law but the assembled crowd believed that, under these singular circumstances, she surely would be freed.

Durham: looking back from the road to the gallows.

However, after only a short consideration, her fate was confirmed; she would be hanged again. The unbending, remorseless and unforgiving demands of the law and the agonies of slow strangulation, it seemed, could not be avoided. It took the best part of an hour for someone to go back into the city, to procure and return with another suitable rope. Twice condemned and twice it seemed reprieved; Mary, now resolved to her ultimate fate, chatted calmly to her distressed friends and awaited her own death.

There were those who murmured against what they saw as the gross injustice surrounding the trial and execution of Mary Nicholson. She had been found guilty of the premeditated murder of a woman she had not intended to kill. Meanwhile the real object of her admitted murderous intention, John Atkinson, had escaped without ever being called to account for whatever enormities he had committed upon Mary. Enormities which had, inevitably it seems, hardened her mind to murder but details of which had never been set out before the court in mitigation for Mary during her trial. She had been sentenced to death only to serve a law-abiding and trusted year in fear that her sentence would be confirmed and in hope that it would be overturned. She had again been spared, this time by a weak rope and, so those around claimed, the intercession of the Almighty.

Her final hour passed as the replacement rope was brought and attached to the gallows. The prisoner was once again made to alight the cart and, without further ado, the tragic Mary Nicholson was, in the words of the *Newcastle Chronicle* of the day, 'launched into eternity amidst the shrieks and distressful cries of the surrounding spectators'.

⚕ BROOMSTICK BRIDGE ⚕

In Barnard Castle, the old County Bridge spans the River Tees under the lofty gaze of Bernard de Baliol's ruined walls.

For years, indeed centuries, the bridge, as its title suggests, served as a thoroughfare between the counties of Durham and Yorkshire. During this time, it saw a constant stream of human traffic including tinkers and traders, wanderers and wayfarers, armies and artisans.

But probably the most unusual activities ever to be seen on the bridge were illicit weddings.

Alexander Hilton was an honourable clerical gentleman who came from an old County Durham family and had held a number of livings within the bishopric, being for a time Rector of Romaldkirk. When he died, he left behind a son, Cuthbert, who was very different from the father. In fact, Cuthbert Hilton

The old County Bridge, Barnard Castle, around 1823.

is recorded as being 'of great notoriety' and, though named after the patron saint of the County Palatine of Durham, Cuthbert Hilton had taken no holy orders and had trained instead as a Bible clerk to his father.

Nonetheless, when the time came, Cuthbert considered himself fully competent and fully qualified to carry out marriage ceremonies. This, admittedly, he did in an unconventional and peculiar way, which was simple in the extreme.

The couple about to be joined in matrimony were escorted by the presiding Cuthbert Hilton to the middle of the County Bridge; no doubt friends followed and any traffic was stopped. Once there, Hilton placed a broomstick across the road and instructed the couple to jump over it together whilst he recited the following doggerel:

> My blessings on your pates,
> And your groats in my purse;
> You are never the better,
> And I'm never the worse.

That was that and, with the marriage ceremony now complete, the satisfied newly-weds happily went on their way while the equally satisfied Cuthbert Hilton departed with his purse hanging heavy about him.

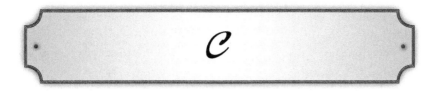

⁜ CONSPIRACY AND CODE ⁑

There in Durham's Gothic shade
His relics are in secret laid;
But none may know the place,
Save of his holiest servants three,
Deep sworn to solemn secrecy,
Who share that wondrous grace.

The above lines were written by Sir Walter Scott and appear in his poem *Marmion*. They refer to an age-old tradition which tells that the body of St Cuthbert does not in fact lie at the spot in Durham Cathedral now familiar to all as his grave. The tradition suggests that the body was moved in the mid-sixteenth century to another place, the location of which remains secret to this day.

The Reformation had arrived in England. Durham Cathedral would be surrendered to Dr Leigh, Dr Henley and Master Blitheman, Commissioners of King Henry VIII. A sledgehammer had crashed down upon the shrine of St Cuthbert, 'One of the most sumptuous in all England', and with that crude blow the age of its splendour had been ended: 'Its treasures stolen away and the body treated with indignity.' The king's officers set about clearing away the myths of antiquity by destroying both the shrine and the sacred reputation of the saint's incorruptibility. No doubt the monks of Durham watched, horrified, as the grave was opened and the body of the great saint was violently disrespected.

If the Commissioners had expected or hoped to find only a skeleton (proving once and for all that the belief in the saint's incorruptibility was nothing more than a superstitious myth), then what they actually found must have disappointed and unnerved them, even causing them to send off for further instructions from a higher authority. For the *Rites of Durham*, written in 1593, relate that the saint's body, over 850 years after his burial, was found to be: 'Whole, uncorrupt, and with his face bare and his beard, as it had been a fortnight's growth, and all his vestments upon him as he was accustomed to say mass, and his metwand of gold lying beside him.'

Instructions came back to the Commissioners that the coffin should be reinterred. The monks of Durham once again laid to rest the body of their saint, covering his now shattered shrine with the simple grey slab we see today. Or did they?

The tradition persists that, fearing further enormities against the holy remains of their patron, they removed St Cuthbert's body and placed in his coffin the bones of another. They then reinterred the saint secretly at some other location within the cathedral, the knowledge of which is said to have been held since that time by the successors of those few conspiratorial monks.

In 1827, however, St Cuthbert's grave was reopened by Revd James Raine. This time no complete body was found; simply a skeleton, of normal proportions, with traces of what appeared to be skin still adhering to bones; disjointed and detached, but undamaged. There was also, rather surprisingly, what appeared to be eyeballs, but which, upon examination, were seen to have been made of 'a mere preparation'. Proof it seemed, for those who looked for it, that the myth of St Cuthbert's incorruptibility had most probably always been just that: a myth.

It has been suggested, however, that, perhaps reflecting the religious mood in the country at the time, Revd Raine had something of his own agenda and wished 'not to confirm his faith, but to establish his scepticism'. And the coffin

St Cuthbert's grave and site of his shrine, destroyed in the Reformation.

exposed by him, dry as a bone itself, told that bones were indeed all that it had ever contained and 'most satisfactorily proved that flesh and blood had never been its inmates'.

Concerns were also raised in some quarters about the way the investigation had been carried out. Why, it was asked, had it been conducted in such a seemingly casual, surreptitious, even secretive way? Comments were made about the fact that only one prebendary of the cathedral had been present, together with a verger and two workmen. Strange, it seemed, for something of such potential importance. Another prebendary had actually been present in the cathedral at the time but was apparently oblivious of the proceedings whilst 'engaged in the services of the choir'. After going to investigate unexpected and unexplained noises, he found the workmen actually trampling around in the saint's grave. Immediately realising the significance of what was happening, he sent off a request for more witnesses to be brought from the city and from Ushaw College before the investigation went any further. Interestingly the sub-dean refused, apparently because he did not want a fuss!

Other doubts were raised. It was revealed that, sometime before the grave was uncovered, an opening had been discovered in the masonry at the end of the burial vault. Apparently this had been filled with loose stones 'which proved that the grave had been opened previously to the investigation'. Had this been done in centuries past or more recently?

Some protesters also insisted that written records detailed how one of the saint's legs had been broken when the sixteenth-century Commissioners flung the contents of the coffin across the floor. The fact that the bones discovered in 1827 were reputedly intact seemed to cast further doubt over whether they really were the bones of the saint. It was also felt to be significant that a linen wrapping cloth, present in the grave at the time of the Commissioners, was not there in 1827. And why it was asked, in the heat of the Reformation, would the Commissioners have even reported what they had found at Durham if it was not true? After all, they were representatives of the new thinking, of the new Church of Henry VIII; it was their business to debunk such superstitious legends of the old order, not to confirm them.

And so the story (unsolved) endures to this day, Scott's lines depicting the conspiracy of those few sixteenth-century monks and the secret of St Cuthbert's *real* burial site. Its location is perhaps known only by those in possession of the Cuthbert Code (a secret, held under solemn oath) and an ancient plan of the cathedral.

And these secret few? Well it has been intimated that they are small in number, possibly only three. That they are members of the Benedictine Order in England and, as such, the direct successors of those original conspiratorial monks who had sworn an oath to keep the secret and to divulge it only before death, to a chosen successor. The secret is thereby being continually passed on 'so long as Christianity should continue to be professed in Durham'.

Alternatively, it has been suggested that there is no sworn oath at all, but that the secret is known generally throughout the Benedictine Order. Or perhaps it is known only by senior members of the Roman Catholic Church; possibly by the Roman Catholic bishops of the Northern Circuit. Or even that the secret is held jointly, perhaps between the Abbot of Ampleforth, the great Benedictine abbey and college in North Yorkshire, and the Archbishop of Westminster, head of the Roman Catholic Church in England and Wales.

Or perhaps the whole thing is just one of those tales that has grown up over centuries of telling!

Interestingly, since the investigation of 1827, surviving pieces of the saint's original, seventh-century coffin have been examined and, using them, the coffin has been partly reconstructed. The reconstruction reveals that to modern eyes it would have been surprisingly small, perhaps suggesting that in life St Cuthbert must have been small in stature. The bones uncovered in 1827 were, however, described as being of normal size, although the exact measurements were not recorded.

One final thing worth considering is the dying wish of St Cuthbert himself and the reason for his body ever coming to Durham. He requested of his monks of Lindisfarne that they bury him on his beloved island, but he also included these words: 'You are to remember that if you are forced to choose between two evils, I would much rather that you lift my bones from the tomb … than that in any way you should consent to evil, and put your necks under the yoke of schismatics.'

Fenwick Lawson's carving of St Cuthbert stands today in the garden of the Durham Museum and Heritage Centre.

So it may be that St Cuthbert's body is interred, not where tradition has it, but lies in a high place and looks to the west. Nevertheless, to all that visit the cathedral today, the bones that lie under that plain, grey marble slab are indeed the bones of the saint. So it should be and so, no doubt, it will remain. The saint's burial place, secret or not, is ultimately still acknowledged to be in the cathedral and accordingly Durham Cathedral is still, and always will be, the shrine of St Cuthbert.

⚜ COPEMAN'S DESPAIR ⚜

The following tale, sometimes told with slight variations, is quite well known around Durham City.

Frederick John Copeman was, according to the story, an early student of Durham University. He resided in Durham Castle, as indeed do today's students of University College. Once the official seat of the prince bishops of Durham, it was given to the university at its foundation by the last prince bishop, William van Mildert, and is today, we are told, the oldest inhabited student residence still in use in Britain.

Copeman was an able, diligent scholar. But, as the time drew near for the release of the final examination results, he became more insular, more agitated; apprehensive, no doubt, but at the same time hopeful about what his final classification would be and what it might lead to. Perhaps launching him towards success and intellectual recognition, the acceptance, even the acclaim of his peers, or perhaps condemning him to academic anonymity. Fellow undergraduates, resident in the castle, would hear him restlessly pacing back and forth in his room high in the castle keep until nervous exhaustion began to take its toll on him.

At last the day of the publication of results arrived and notices setting out the names of candidates and their final classifications were placed in a glass-fronted wooden display case on the wall of what is today Palace Green Library. And it was there that anxious undergraduates made their way in order to establish their fate. When the word spread that the results were out, Copeman clattered breathlessly out of his door, dashed down the stairs, ran across the castle courtyard and out through the gateway; there to join the

Castle keep, today's home of University College, Durham.

Exterior of the Great Hall, Durham Castle.

throng of his fellow scholars. Some he observed laughing the laughter of relief and achievement, while others stood in the silence and reflection of what could or should have been.

Frederick John Copeman scanned the notices, his eyes skimming across the lists of names, but without seeing his own. He looked again, carefully this time. Surely he was there somewhere! But still he could see no reference to his result. At length, the awful truth dawned on him; his name wasn't there amongst the names of the successful. He must have failed his final examinations. Failed to graduate; failed totally. And in that awful moment of realisation, he saw his destiny and silently turned away from those hateful notices.

In the clamour and excitement of the day, nobody saw Copeman much after that. Quietly he stole back to the castle keep, where some of his fellow students said they heard him, pacing monotonously back and forth across his room. What was he to do? Eventually he was resolved and quietly he left the castle, walked calmly across the courtyard and through the gateway. Averting his eyes from the scene of his despair, he made for the cathedral, entering it through the great North Door. Looking for the peace of mind or the spiritual salvation which only

Today's students at a matriculation ceremony.

that venerable place could give him? Perhaps. Seeking the solace of the saints? Well, that may have been so. But nobody noticed him as he began to ascend the 325 steps to the quiet solitude atop the central tower, nor did they notice as he approached the edge of those holy heights, throwing himself to his death.

Unbeknown to the tragic Frederick John Copeman, when the results had first been posted, his own had indeed been there but had slipped down behind another and were therefore hidden from his searching eyes. Copeman had passed his final examinations and had achieved a First.

Many students of University College have matriculated and graduated since Frederick John Copeman, but the story tells that often since his fateful day, footsteps have been heard pacing the boards of his old room, which incidentally ceased to be used as accommodation, eventually becoming simply a storeroom.

Or so, at least, the story tells!

❖ CUTTY THROAT FARM ❖

The Devil made me do it!

So claimed the protagonist in one of the most brutal and shocking murder cases ever witnessed in County Durham; a case that caused outrage, even by the standards of the time in which it took place. It would eventually be given a life of its own in a theatrical melodrama, played to packed houses at the Spennymoor Theatre some two centuries after the event and exaggerating a horror which needed no exaggeration. So terrible was this case that it is still embedded in the local consciousness over 300 years later.

John and Margaret Brass worked a farm, high up on the ridge between Ferryhill and Kirk Merrington. They had three children: Elizabeth, aged 11, John, 17, and the eldest, Jane, who was almost 20 years old and shortly to be married. They also employed as a servant a local youth, Andrew Mills. At about 19 years old, he was described as being perhaps a little slow-witted and childlike but good-natured and a willing worker.

On the evening of Thursday, 25 January 1683, John and Margaret were returning to their farm after visiting friends when suddenly Mills dashed out of the darkness in front of their horse and stared at them with wild eyes, before turning away and disappearing into the night. Instinctively knowing that something was dreadfully wrong, they hurried back to their farm where, to their horror, they found all their children dead. The alarm was raised and it wasn't long before Andrew Mills was detained at Ferryhill by a troop of soldiers who happened to be passing between Darlington and Durham City that very night. He was hysterical and covered in blood. Charged with the murder of the Brass children, Mills duly appeared in court in Durham City. No real motive for the killings could be established, but the nature of his confession, recorded by the Durham diarist, Jacob Bee, was sensational.

The night was drawing on when the normally good-natured boy had become very angry; he could not explain why. In his sudden fury, he had picked up an axe and attacked the eldest daughter, Jane. She fled from his murderous strokes and barricaded herself inside the bedroom, where the other two children were sleeping. Mills smashed at the door with his axe until the wooden bolt shattered and Jane, in desperation, thrust her forearm into the door staples to replace it. But Mills continued his relentless onslaught until the door broke open and flew back, breaking Jane's arm. He then set about his bloody business.

He quickly despatched Jane and her brother and turned to the child, Elizabeth. She pleaded with him, offering him sweets and toys. At this Mills seemed to relent, turning away from her and shuffling out into the corridor. But there, so he told, he was confronted by a horror. Something evil stood in the shadows. The devil, in the form of a hideous creature, 'with fiery eyes and eagle's wings', commanded him: 'go back thou hateful wretch, resume thy cursed work. I long to view more blood, spare not the young one's life; kill all, kill all.' Mills turned, went back into the bedroom, and duly murdered little Elizabeth.

Found guilty of the terrible crimes, Mills went to the gallows on Wednesday, 15 August 1683. He was then 'Hanged in irons upon a gybett' at the spot where he had encountered the children's parents that terrible night. This spot, according to the *Monthly Chronicle*, stood 'about a mile and a half north of Ferryhill', on the

Great North Road and looked across and up to the scene of his dreadful deeds. Of course the site of Andrew Mills' Stob, as the gibbet became known, quickly acquired an evil reputation. Local people did all they could to avoid passing it, especially at night and, over the centuries, a plethora of local folklore built up around it.

The Brass children were buried in Kirk Merrington churchyard and a table monument was erected by public subscription in 1789. It can still be seen today with the following words now faint, but still just visible:

> Reader remember, sleeping
> we were slain;
> And here we sleep till we must
> rise again;
> Who so sheddeth man's blood, by man shall
> his blood be shed.
> Thou shalt do no murder.

Eventually, in the 1830s, the land upon which Andrew Mills' Stob stood was bought by a Mr Laverick, who ploughed up the site. As for the stump of the gibbet pole, the *Monthly Chronicle* tells that Mr Laverick 'removed it bodily – reports sayeth not where'. With the removal of Andrew Mills' Stob, it would perhaps have been

Kirk Merrington church, with the memorial to the Brass children in the foreground.

The table monument erected by public subscription in 1789.

'Reader remember, sleeping we were slain.'

thought that that would be the end of the whole tragic episode: 'The most horrid and barbarous murder that ever was heard in the North or elsewhere.'

However, it has been suggested to the author that stories continued to circulate about queer goings-on at the Black & Decker factory, at Thinford; not far from the spot where Andrew Mills was hung in chains. Odd, inexplicable, apparently uncanny incidents would occur, bringing a sense of unease to the workers affected by them. And sometimes, for no apparent reason, day-to-day operations failed to go smoothly, as unforeseen problems suddenly arose. Naturally, most were reluctant to suggest a haunting as an explanation for the seemingly mysterious events, much less to raise the spectre of the long-dead Andrew Mills. But others, knowing the history of the area, privately ascribed the incidents to the doings of his unquiet spirit. Of course, the incidents may just have been industrial gremlins at work, or perhaps even simply the product of urban myth.

A brand new regeneration development, the Durham Gate, has now grown up on the same site. It is apparently, at the time of writing, nearing completion. But it has been subject to delay. In fact, according to press reports, the development has failed to go smoothly and unforeseen problems have suddenly arisen.

So the tortured soul of Andrew Mills may well still be at large. Perhaps someone, somewhere, in the new, flagship development, will experience something odd, inexplicable and apparently uncanny.

Time will tell.

⁘ DEATH COACH ⁘

Death omens, portents of the impending doom of individuals, are a familiar supernatural motif. They come in different guises: from the fetch, the apparition or likeness of a living person that appears usually but not uniquely to relatives just before or at the point of that person's death; to the celebrated Irish banshees, the sad, phantom maidens whose heart-rending wailing lament presaged a death in the particular family to which they were historically attached; and the Scottish *bean nighe*, who was sometimes seen washing the bloodied shirts of those about to die a violent death.

County Durham has its own death omen and can boast of the large black horse that allegedly arose from Tudhoe Village pond (when Tudhoe Village had a pond) before the death of a local resident. The horse was then walked up and down the village by a headless rider. Many witnessed it, apparently, including the village blacksmith, his grandfather, father, three sons and two daughters, all of whom claimed to have seen it arise at midnight and only return to its watery abode before the break of day. John Hickson and Neddy Hunt, 'two hangers-on' at the blacksmith's shop, also claimed to have seen it more than once, 'but never durst approach it'. It is perhaps cynical to suggest that at least some of the sightings may have had more to do with a good night spent at The Green Tree public house.

In St Mary's churchyard, Barnard Castle, on the side of the tomb of one George Hopper, 'Gentleman, Died 1795', is carved the skeletal figure of death, complete with his scythe. It is said that if the scythe is seen to move it portends the certain death of the beholder, or one of his family. Of the gentlemanly George Hopper, nothing is known.

However, more spectacular perhaps than all of the above are the death coaches, or spectral hearses, which appeared to those about to die, and are a dark, familiar theme, figuring widely in ghost lore.

William Brockie, in his book *Legends & Superstitions of the County of Durham*, published in 1886, relates a tale that he was told by a Mr George Gamsby. The curious event that had been the origin of the story had taken place in the time of that gentleman's grandmother. One night, a fearful noise was heard all down Silver Street in Durham, sounding as if it was made by 'a horse with a lame foot and chain attached to it, but exaggerated twenty times, for the whole street was shaken, as it might have been with an earthquake'. Some stout-hearted citizens plucked up the courage to look out from their upstairs windows in order to witness the cause of the unholy din. What they beheld was 'something like a stagecoach, drawn by six horses', with 'a lot of men on the top'. The coach, the men and the horses; all were black. Curiously, the witnesses could not tell whether the vision moved up the street or down it.

Coaches in Silver Street, Durham City.

In any collection of good ghost stories there will be found tales of spectral black coaches; sometimes seen, sometimes heard, sometimes both. Perhaps witnessed clattering up the driveways of great houses, accompanied by a great rushing, terrifying noise or sometimes even, and perhaps more alarmingly, indoors; silently ascending staircases. Invariably these spectral coaches are driven manically by a coachman who is usually headless and dressed in black, or occasionally appears as a skeleton-like figure. The phantom coaches are commonly pulled by black steeds, usually horses, though sometimes they appear, rather curiously, to be pulled by swine. These swine are also almost always headless, though sometimes described, rather oddly considering their condition, as breathing fire through their nostrils.

A phantom coach, pulled by 'black and fiery steeds', was often reported driving at breakneck speed, rapidly but noiselessly 'along the rough approach to Langley Hall', near Durham. The driver of this particular coach, conforming to tradition, was headless, as were his steeds.

Such reports have been assigned to the realms of ghost folklore, usually with a backstory of some wicked person paying the price for their misdeeds in life, causing the phantom coach to whisk their soul away to spend eternity in damnation or perhaps returning them to the scene of their earthly infamy on the anniversary of their death. Nothing more, then, than a dark folk fantasy? Well, perhaps not always.

John Borrow was a regular at the ale houses of seventeenth-century Durham City. One winter's night he made his way up Silver Street to the Market Place, from where, so he claimed, he witnessed coming towards him from the direction of Claypath a black coach, driven by a black driver, and pulled by black steeds. The steeds were of the porcine, rather than the equine, variety though in this instance they were complete with heads; as, it seems, was the driver. This nonetheless terrifying vision made its way across the Market Place towards Saddler Street and simply vanished. Of course, others were sceptical about his claims; nobody else had seen anything strange, or at least anything stranger than usual for Durham Market Place. Borrows' wild claim was put down to intoxication and a vivid imagination and he was generally disbelieved. Soon after, however, Borrow died.

The curious case of John Borrow was recorded in a very matter-of-fact entry by the Durham diarist, Jacob Bee:

17 January, 1685.

Departed this life John Borrow of Durham.

It was reported yt he see a coach drawn by six swine, all black, and a black man satt upon the cotch box; he fell sick upon't and dyed.

❧ DOCTOR STIRLING'S MURDER ❧

There is a report on the Paranormal Database website which tells of the occasional appearance in woodland near Rowland's Gill of two ghostly figures 'with pale faces and bright eyes'. There can also be heard nearby a dreadful eerie moaning, as if made by someone in their death throes. Perhaps taken together they are a phantom reminder, or an imprint on the landscape, of a dreadful crime committed in the mid-nineteenth century 'in a lonely road called Smailes Lane, about a mile north of the village of Burnopfield'.

Early in November 1855, a letter arrived at the home of a respectable Scottish family. Sent from County Durham, it told them of the sudden disappearance of their beloved son. Perhaps as a direct consequence of the letter, the son's mother then had a terrible dream. In it she saw her boy brutally murdered on a lonely road, far from help and far from home. Following the letter and the woman's nightmarish vision, her husband set off at once to establish exactly what had happened.

Young Dr Robert Stirling was 26 years of age and only recently arrived from Kirkintilloch in Dunbartonshire, but he was already establishing himself as an able assistant to Dr William Watson of Burnopfield. He was popular with his patients and, after borrowing a silver pocket watch from a colleague, he set out to visit them at 9 a.m. on 1 November. However, Dr Stirling failed to return; it seemed that he had simply disappeared. An alarmed Dr Watson soon alerted the authorities and quickly sent off a letter to Dr Stirling's parents.

A search was begun and Dr Stirling's father eventually arrived from Scotland to assist with it. Five full days were to elapse, however, before the young doctor was found. His body was discovered hidden in a thicket of woodland high above the River Derwent and it was instantly obvious that he had been murdered. His money and the silver pocket watch were gone but most frightful of all was the manner in which he had been killed: he had been shot, his throat cut and his head and face battered in, 'apparently by the butt end of a gun'. Tragically fate decreed that it was the father who, with two other men, found the body of his own dead son, witnessing at first hand the terrible injuries that had been inflicted upon him and confirming as dreadful reality the dark dream of his wife. There quickly followed an investigation by the authorities and a reward for information was offered.

Ralph Stobart was a drover from Cumberland who had been visiting his sister for a few days and, on the morning of 1 November, had begun his journey back home. Making his way along Smailes Lane, he noticed two men loitering near a thicket of trees. Not liking the look of them, he hurried on by and shortly afterwards he passed a young man coming in the opposite direction, to whom he spoke, and who returned his pleasantries with a noticeable Scottish accent. This was the last time Dr Stirling was seen alive.

Another man, a tenant of the Gibside Estate, was due to travel down the same road that morning at his regular hour; 1 November being rent day. However, he always feared this particular journey, as the area was often frequented by thieves and ruffians who lay in wait along the road. In fact, the previous night he'd had a disturbing dream that had left him with an indistinct but nonetheless alarming feeling of threat. The dream, or nightmare, seemed to be a warning that something was going to happen to him on that very journey the next morning. So real was it that, after discussing it with his wife, he decided to break with his regular routine and set off much earlier; an action that may well have saved his life.

Information eventually came to light that the two men seen in the vicinity of Smailes Lane on 1 November had been recognised as John 'Whiskey Jack' Kane, a distiller of illicit whiskey and known to the authorities, and Richard Raine, a local blacksmith. Whisky Jack and Richard Raine were duly arrested and put on trial for murder. Local people firmly believed that the pair were guilty as charged, the popular theory being that they had in fact been lying in wait for the tenant carrying his rent money. Certainly it was known that Kane held a grudge against the man since some time earlier, the self-same tenant having given information against him to the Revenue. Doctor Stirling, it seemed, had tragically been in the wrong place at the wrong time. Appearing first at the 1856 Spring Assizes in Durham City, the evidence against Kane and Raine was damning but incomplete and the pair were remanded for the Summer Assizes, in July.

Mrs Stirling claimed that in her dream she had seen the face of her son's murderer. In light of this, a request was made to the governor of Durham Gaol, for her to visit and if possible confirm the killer's identity. The request was granted, Mrs Stirling travelled down from Scotland and a line-up of prisoners was arranged for her to see. Without hesitation, Mrs Stirling pointed straight at Whisky Jack Kane. However, convincing as this may have seemed to the local population, by the mid-nineteenth century the contents of a dream did not constitute evidence in a courtroom.

The trial began on 25 July 1856, when, before Mr Justice Willis, the accused men pleaded not guilty. During the proceedings, Ralph Stobart, the Cumberland drover, testified that he had seen two men loitering in Smailes Lane and said that one of them seemed to carrying a gun or a stick. Shortly after his meeting with Dr Stirling, further along the same lane, he had heard what he thought was a gunshot. Crucially, however, he could not be certain that the two men in the dock were the same two men he had seen on that fateful day.

Both Kane and Raine had also been seen in Durham City, shortly after the murder. Raine had offered a silver pocket watch to a pawnbroker, who would not advance him anything on it. Putting the watch back in his pocket, Raine turned tail and left and a potentially vital piece of evidence, which may have linked the two men directly to the murder, was lost. As it was, the evidence against the pair was purely circumstantial and it could not be proved conclusively that they had indeed committed the murder. After a two-day trial and a deliberation of two and a half hours, the jury found them not guilty. Whisky Jack Kane and Robert Raine were both set free. It seemed a bitter injustice for the parents of Dr Stirling.

What became of the silver pocket watch would never be known, though word went round after the trial that Raine had thrown it from one of Durham City's bridges into the River Wear below. Nobody else ever stood trial for the brutal murder of young Dr Stirling and it was later written of the case that this was 'one of the most cold blooded, dastardly, and foulest murders recorded in our criminal annals, and must remain as an unpunished crime'.

According to the Paranormal Database, the phantom figures began to be witnessed and the dreadful ghostly sounds began to be heard around fifteen years after the terrible events took place. Perhaps they continue to this day; a ghostly reminder of a grave injustice.

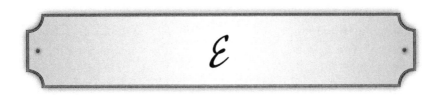

❧ EBCHESTER'S BURNING MAN ❧

The evangelist, religious reformer and founder of the Methodist Church, John Wesley, was a frequent visitor to County Durham. Journeying on horseback across bleak moorland, in all weather and well into his old age, Wesley's main areas of ministry were Weardale, where he described the Stanhope of his day as being 'eminent for nothing in this age but a very uncommon degree of wickedness', and Teesdale, where he was initially chased from Barnard Castle by men who brought out the town's water engine and 'Showered down their blessings upon his head'. During his regular visits to County Durham between 1742 and 1790, he was told the following tale of an incident which occurred at Ebchester; the site of Vindomora, County Durham's most northern Roman fort on the Dere Street road.

The year was 1737 and in Ebchester, Cuthbert Johnson had just married without the consent of his father, Robert. So offended was Robert Johnson that, immediately making out his will, he bequeathed absolutely nothing to his son. On no account, he vowed, would Cuthbert receive anything; no money, land, nor property. In addition, Robert wished that 'his right arm might be burnt off if he failed to keep his vow'.

But time, so they say, is a great healer. Years passed, circumstances changed and father and son were reconciled. Robert, changing his will shortly before he died, now left everything to Cuthbert.

Before being placed in the coffin and taken for burial, Robert's body had been laid out with appropriate dignity in a room of the family home, giving loved ones a chance to pay their last respects. The assembled relatives, however, suddenly became aware of 'a disagreeable smell' emanating from the room in which Robert's body lay. Dashing in, they were confronted with a dreadful sight. The whole room was full of smoke and, to their horror, they witnessed flames bursting from the dead man's body, which they could plainly see was 'slowly smouldering'. They could also see that, curiously, the right arm 'was practically burned off'.

Hurriedly depositing and sealing the body in the coffin, 'from whence immediately afterwards, a noise of burning and crackling was heard', the horrified relatives hastened from the scene of this grim drama to the graveyard of Ebchester church. Once there, they deposited the mortal remains of Robert Johnson without further delay.

So the tale was told to John Wesley and so it has been handed down.

Wesley, however, probably added a few extra details, erroneous or not, in his own diary account of the incident. He tells that Johnson's body was buried 'near the steeple of the church' and that, alarmingly, as the burial was taking place, the funeral party witnessed the steeple shake. Then, no more than two minutes after, part of it collapsed and the mourners narrowly escaped death. Perhaps Wesley was simply adding a symbolic veneer to the events, to serve as a further warning of the retribution meted out to those who swore dark oaths.

Spontaneous human combustion is a controversial and little understood phenomenon, if truly it is understood at all. Exactly how *spontaneous* it is remains the subject of debate. There are a number of theories as to its actual cause and the mechanics of its progress but none of these have yet met with universal acceptance. The terrible and inevitably fatal effects of it are real enough, however, and not, as some believe, an urban myth. Indeed there are numerous accounts of its victims, their bodies either partially or totally consumed by a fire which had obviously burned at an exceptionally high temperature yet paradoxically left unburned, and even uncharred, surrounding furniture, fittings and even clothing worn by the victim.

Tragic indeed! However, not fatal in the curious case of Robert Johnson, as he was most assuredly dead before his body combusted.

⚜ ELEVATED ⚜

The great medieval Prince Bishops of Durham were extremely powerful and influential men. They ruled virtually independently of the king, upheld their own laws, minted their own money and led their own armies. Sir Timothy Eden, in his book *County Durham*, tells us that some of these individuals were 'among the most splendidly arrogant figures in English history'. Not least of their number was Thomas Hatfield.

A warrior ecclesiastic, Hatfield was Prince Bishop of Durham from 1345 to 1381, ably fulfilling his dual role and office, both as bishop and spiritual head of the Bishopric of Durham, the ancient Patrimony of St Cuthbert; and as Count Palatine, the civil and military ruler of the county. For a bishop of the Church, Hatfield was considered 'rather light on religious qualifications', but his political influence and secular roles were both impressive and important. Close advisor and secretary to the all-powerful King Edward III, Hatfield was also keeper of the privy seal, counsellor to the king's son and commander of the king's armies. In fact, he fought alongside Edward at the Battle of Crécy and at the Siege of Calais.

The haughty Hatfield, described by the chronicler William Chambre as proud, ambitious and overbearing, may well have shown due deference to his liege lord, the mighty Edward III, but he paid little heed to those who would be his ecclesiastical masters, to the English archbishops, and even to the Pope.

The bishop's throne, the cathedra, 'The Highest Throne in Christendom'?

Indeed, in his dealings with the Archbishop of York we are told that Hatfield 'maintained the animosity common to his forebears', publishing a protest and declaring his complete exemption from obedience or subjection to the archbishop. Appalled, the archbishop planned a visit to Durham in 1376 to demand ecclesiastical obedience from Hatfield but was told, by King Edward himself, not to do so, 'it being likely to promote disturbance'.

Eventually, Hatfield, 'ever tenacious of rank, impatient of control and conscious of his own importance', decided that his seat of authority at Durham, his cathedra (the bishop's throne in Durham Cathedral), needed improving to something perhaps more befitting the exalted status of a Prince Bishop of Durham. To this end, he sent off emissaries and craftsmen to Rome, with the instruction to examine the nature of the Pope's own throne. They were especially ordered to make note of its height. On their return to Durham, Hatfield ordered the alterations that he considered necessary to be made, and his cathedra was built up to be higher than the Pope's in Rome; not by much, but just by enough. From that day on it was claimed that the prince bishop's throne in Durham Cathedral was indeed 'The Highest Throne in Christendom' and the imperious Thomas Hatfield was eventually buried under it and lies there to this day.

Bishop Hatfield's tomb, Durham Cathedral.

It is said, in a tale which may well be apocryphal, that, when the Pope heard of what Hatfield had done, he afterwards simply sat on a cushion.

⋅❈ FINKLE ❈⋅

Finchale Priory, a few short miles from Durham City, stands on an ancient Christian site. It is thought that, in the years AD 792 and 810, early Church Synods were held there and also that Anglo-Saxon Councils (Witans) gathered at the same place, then called Wincanhale. We are also told that it was the scene of the death, in AD 765, of Ethelward, King of Northumbria. However, the site is most associated with St Godric, the pirate saint, who settled there in the twelfth century. For many years Godric lived a life of prayer and meditation and his isolated abode at Finchale became a place of pilgrimage for the faithful. Suffering the privations of Scottish raids and sometimes praying all through the night whilst standing waist deep in the River Wear, Godric fought his own spiritual war against the forces of evil, until his life of devotion finally ended at the alleged great age of 105. After his death, a monastery was built around his burial site.

In later years, Finchale became a cell of the great Benedictine priory of Durham Cathedral; a retreat and place of relaxation for the Durham monks. But scurrilous stories began to circulate about the exact nature of the relaxation enjoyed since monastic discipline, so the stories hinted, had become rather loose. In addition to the more obvious ascetic delights of their peaceful, spiritual idyll, the monks, it seems, liked to indulge in more worldly pastimes: holding their own hunts and greatly enjoying the pleasures of the chase. Indeed, the Prior of Durham himself was obliged to reprimand the Finchale brethren for keeping their own pack of hounds. Other rumours also persisted, such as the healing properties of the Prior of Finchale's chair. Rumours became oft-repeated stories which, in turn, became commonly held beliefs; beliefs that the monkish community of Finchale did little to dispel, it seems.

The chair, known as the Wishing Chair, was said to have the miraculous power to make barren women fertile. Writing in the eighteenth century, the antiquary, Francis Grose, tells us that 'it was said to have the virtue of removing sterility and procuring issue for any woman who, having performed certain ceremonies, sat down therein'. Grose adds, rather pointedly, 'it may perhaps be needless to observe that since the removal of the monks, it has entirely lost its efficacy'.

Finchale Priory across the River Wear.

Later still came the Reformation. Monastic establishments were dissolved and the old ways abolished. The new ways were quickly seized upon by the last Prior of Finchale, William Bennett, who, clearly taking the view that the Dissolution released him from his monastic vows, took the opportunity to marry. This in turn led a contemporary commentator to pronounce: 'The Prior of Finkel hath got a fair wife, and now every monk will have one.'

Around 400 years then passed before curious reports began to circulate about the now ruined Finchale Priory and its environs; stories from unnamed witnesses and whispers of something strange. There were tales of mysterious, dark, ephemeral figures seen moving around during the night-time and of alarming encounters with an unpleasant, limping, hunchbacked entity, thought to be the ghost of a monk. These encounters apparently happened so frequently that the ghost was even given a name: Slewfoot. Of course, if a ruined priory is going to be haunted at all, then for it to be haunted by the ghost of a monk is perhaps a logical and unsurprising state of events, if perhaps slightly unimaginative.

However, other, perhaps more exotic reports from Finchale tell of what appear to be instances of time slips. Most witnesses to (or victims of) these odd phenomena have apparently attested that their experience occurred in the vicinity of, or whilst actually standing on, the footbridge.

'Time Slip' bridge.

First built in 1925, the bridge leads away from the priory ruins, over the river, to Cocken Wood. Usually, the sudden descent of a curiously heavy and stifling atmosphere, accompanied by the onset of an inexplicable feeling of intense melancholy and a sense of otherworldliness, presages a brief vision of

Finchale Priory ruins around 1887.

modern-day buildings being replaced by those of an earlier age, and the priory appearing, not as it now is, but as it once was. Unfortunately, reports are vague and witnesses unnamed, which may perhaps suggest to the reader that they are just good stories, and the reports, perhaps even the witnesses themselves, no more than urban myth.

Interestingly, Sir Timothy Eden, writing in the mid-twentieth century, perhaps offers an oblique reference to the phenomena. On his visit to a nearby site he describes: 'Standing in the wilderness of what was once a garden … I wished that I had the gift of vision of those good ladies who saw the vanished beauties of Versailles.' This seems to allude to a famous alleged time slip incident in August 1901, when Charlotte Anne Moberly and Eleanor Jourdain, Principal and Vice Principal of St Hugh's College, Oxford, apparently experienced a time slip in the gardens of the Petit Trianon at the Palace of Versailles. Reporting sudden feelings of sadness and the descent of a strange, sullen atmosphere on what had been a vibrant sunny day, they witnessed the somewhat neglected buildings suddenly change to what must have been their former glory, from a former age, with people going about their business dressed in the clothing of a time before the French Revolution.

Unfortunately, on this occasion, no such vision was granted to Sir Timothy, as he concludes rather sadly: 'but I saw nothing but weeds.'

❖ FRANCHISE ❖

Early in the nineteenth century, despite the rapid growth of the working population of Spennymoor, the town had only seven electors; six Conservatives and one Liberal.

In the early days, the Liberal Party struggled, sometimes in vain, to overturn the political balance. During one election a cab was sent to collect the sole Liberal voter, Mr Thomas Byers, who was apparently so embarrassed at the prospect of being its solitary occupant that, for appearance's sake, he made his young son travel with him: 'I took our Will, to make the cab look decent.'

But the course of decades can change a political landscape and James J. Dodd, writing in 1897, tells us that: 'Spennymoor has always taken a keen interest in the fortunes of the Liberal Party.' So it was that during the General Election of 1874, followers of prime minister and leader of the Liberal Party, William Gladstone, had become so enthusiastic in their support that they brought about a state of affairs never before (and probably never since) seen in that town.

On the day of the election, a very canny Conservative agent, no doubt demonstrating his loyalty to party leader Benjamin Disraeli, intercepted a number of cabs which had been hired from Durham City, at considerable expense, by the

Liberal Party, to take their voters to the poll. This enterprising individual then plastered the vehicles all over with Conservative election posters and used them to take his own supporters to vote.

Perhaps rumour of this 'outrage' had circulated, or perhaps it was just that the mood of Liberal supporters on the day was 'mischievous', but a riot ensued on the streets of Spennymoor. It started innocuously enough with some individuals throwing empty baskets from the railway bridge. These were then kicked around the streets by the gathering malcontents. But the mood quickly blackened and 'the youths became so unusually excited that they lost all control of themselves'. Windows of known Conservative supporters were smashed and when, horror of horrors, the publicans closed their hostelries and barricaded their doors shut, the mob ran up and down the street overturning vehicles and 'dealing destruction right and left'.

In the quiet tranquillity of the Crown Hotel, the only hostelry still open, customers were peacefully imbibing and conversing, oblivious to the wrath of the descending mob, 'When the first stone came in through the window and knocked a glass clean out of a woman's hand, leaving her nothing but the handle'. In a different room, Mr John Brown had his back to the window when his pint was knocked over by another incoming missile. Turning around upon hearing the smashing of glass and seeing his beer spilling across the table, Brown grabbed a fellow drinker by the throat and, mistakenly, accused the man of the crime. Unsurprisingly, the accusation was 'vigorously denied' and the two were just about to begin a 'meaningful exchange' when a veritable hail of missiles crashed in, and, as his customers hastily dived for cover, the landlord of the Crown hastily barricaded his doors shut. And so, as Dodd related, 'it may be said that for the first and only time on record, all the public houses in Spennymoor were closed', a state in which they remained, presumably, until polling had finished.

As for the rest of this eventful, if curious, election day in 1874, supporters of the Liberal Party probably wondered why their cabs had never arrived; and the mood of the youthful rioters was no doubt not lifted when the election result was finally known. For the Liberal Party had lost; Benjamin Disraeli was the new, Conservative, prime minister.

✤ GALA DAY ✤

In July 1925, the annual Miners' Gala, the 'Big Meeting', was held in Durham City. Pitmen and their families from all across the County Durham coalfield had come in their tens of thousands, filling the narrow streets to bursting point before spilling out onto the Racecourse for their day of enjoyment and relaxation in the fresh air and perhaps, occasionally for July, in the sunshine.

But the atmosphere in 1925 was tense. The miners were locked in an ongoing struggle for decent pay and better working conditions and guest speakers stoked the fires of unrest until the mood of the assembled masses was completely uncompromising. To make matters worse they lacked the support of the Bishop of Durham, whose public endorsement they had relied on in years gone by. In fact, the incumbent bishop even went so far as to state publicly that they deserved no pay increase at all.

The bishop had been enthroned in 1920, the same year the Durham Miners had been on strike, demanding a living wage and, amongst other things, a reduction in the price of coal to the consumer. In his inaugural address, His Grace had denounced strikes, stating that: 'I desire my words shall come to every corner of my Diocese, that strikes and lockouts are methods which ought to become obsolete.' Strong words indeed, given the circumstances, but this particular bishop was on record as saying that he cared not about his popularity. Clearly then the historical fact that a previous bishop, William van Mildert,

Durham Miner's Gala, the Riverbanks.

A miners' banner on Big Meeting Day.

had been burned in effigy outside Auckland Castle for publicly opposing the Great Reform Act, would be of no significance to him.

He had, nonetheless, found time to launch a public appeal to 'all patriotic Englishmen' for donations towards the £150,000 needed to carry out essential repair works to Durham Castle. After a 'disappointing' initial response and as a crippled country headed inexorably towards a general strike, the bishop declared that he was 'completely baffled by the indifference of the public'. He denounced the 'drift towards communistic sentiment' and bemoaned that 'England has ceased to be a constitutional monarchy and is making its first advance towards the dictatorship of the proletariat'. Clearly, none of these sentiments did anything to endear him to the Durham miners.

So it was that on a fine July day, a group of pitmen, worse the wear for an afternoon's drinking, noticed a clerical gentleman, sporting a silk top hat and carrying a brolly, strolling along the riverside, lost in his own thoughts and keeping well clear of the crowds. It was the bishop! Here was a golden opportunity for them to wreak their revenge. They rushed at him, grabbed him, and without further hesitation went to throw him into the river. In went the hat, in went the brolly. Fortunately for the helpless gentleman, however, assistance arrived just in time, in the form of a number of police officers and a motor launch, and the clerical gentleman was thus ultimately saved from a soaking. He was released, shocked and bewildered but at least undamaged, apart that is, from a slight loss of dignity. But the angry men had made their point; even the Bishop of Durham could expect no quarter when standing against the Durham Miners.

But on that particular July day in 1925, the Bishop of Durham was in fact safe, secure and comfortably far away from the gathering of hostile miners. The clerical gentleman, who had been so unceremoniously manhandled, was not the bishop but Mr J.E.C. Welldon, the Dean of Durham, who had been there to address a temperance meeting on the subject of 'The Evils of Drink'. Though saddened by the loss of his silk top hat and his umbrella, and no doubt by the irony of the situation, it is not known whether Dean Welldon was ever enlightened as to why such an enormity had been committed against him; or if the vengeful miners ever realised their mistake.

⁜ GONE FISHING ⁜

This short piece concerns five fishermen and an errant pig. The fishermen are described as follows; the pig will be dealt with later.

Nineteenth-century County Durham was well served with notable anglers, particularly exponents of fly-fishing. It may be the case therefore that all, or at least some of the gentlemen remembered below, are already familiar to readers who themselves practice that contemplative craft. Some, if not all, of these fishermen of repute were also known to each other and they spent a great amount of time, both individually and in each other's company, fishing all across County Durham and Northumberland.

William Greenwell, FRS, magistrate and chairman of the petty sessions, was born in Lanchester on 23 March 1820. He was also a minor canon of Durham Cathedral, chapter librarian and a tutor at Durham University's Hatfield Hall. Described as being 'small in stature but with a large head, somewhat resembling the portraits of Darwin', the learned Greenwell was also an eminent archaeologist, antiquarian and author, as well as an enthusiastic fly-fisherman. He was especially noted for inventing very effective artificial fishing flies, still in use today, including the Greenwell salmon-fly and most famous of all, the trout-fly, the Greenwell's Glory. Made originally of blackbird feathers and pale yellow silk, this 'gaily dressed' and apparently irresistible insect was, as any fly-fishermen reading these words will of course know, a fanciful representation of the natural fly, the Olive Dun. Another William, William Henderson, was born in 1813 at Kirk Merrington into an influential business family. He later moved to Durham City and became mayor in 1849. An author of some ability, Henderson penned his own trout and salmon fishing journal as well as a number of works on local folklore.

These two men were joined by a number of others including: Charlie Ebdy, a Durham boat builder who lived at Paradise House, later known as Brown's Boat House; Walter Scruton, a Durham solicitor, who invented the Durham Ranger salmon-fly; and Captain of Militia Percival S. Wilkinson, of Mount Oswald, inventor of the Wilkinson salmon-fly. Together they fished all across County Durham and Northumberland, had great sport and sometimes, by today's reckoning, had incredible catches. Henderson recorded that, over Easter 1836, he, Ebdy and another companion caught 575 trout between them. Several years later, in July 1917, Greenwell went on a three-week fishing trip to North Sunderland. Now in his 98th year, he recorded a haul of 400 perch, ninety eels and six trout. This particular tale, however, concerns a catch of a somewhat different nature, which took place while Henderson and Ebdy were fishing at Sunderland Bridge.

Deciding to partake of some refreshment at the local hostelry, they left their rods leaning against the parapet of the Old Bridge, with Ebdy's bait of worms still attached to the hook. Not long afterwards an apparently itinerant pig just happened to pass by and take an immediate interest in the wriggling morsel on the end of Ebdy's line. Answering the call of its innate curiosity and greed, the pig duly took the bait, and was well and truly hooked. A shout went up and the resting anglers rushed back to their rods. What happened next would later be recorded by Henderson in his journal.

Fishing at Eastgate Linns, Weardale.

Ebdy picked up his rod and the line tightened on his porcine prey. In response, the startled pig shot off at speed across the Old Bridge, with Ebdy (half-chasing, half-playing the animal like a prize salmon) in hot pursuit.

This absurdly comic scenario then entered the realm of pure slapstick when 'a cur of low degree' appeared on the scene, saw what was happening and decided to help by grabbing the animal by its back legs and trying to wrestle it to the ground. But he failed. Succeeding only in enraging the poor pig, which 'vigorously resisted' his assailant's fumbling efforts, he was left bruised, battered and defeated. Eventually breaking free, the animal, 'evidently in excellent racing condition', then made off at a good pace up Croxdale Bank. In pursuit was both the cur, still intent on ultimate victory, and Charlie Ebdy, still playing his catch. And so, Henderson tells us, 'Away went Charlie, the pig and the cur', until at last Ebdy, giving up the chase, snapped his line: 'leaving poor piggy and the cur in full gallop towards Darlington.'

And so it was that between them, these men fished the waters of the County Palatine and beyond throughout the nineteenth century. When Henderson died in November 1891, Canon Greenwell conducted his funeral service and, in 1900, Greenwell himself reflected sadly on an age which he realised had gone for ever. It is interesting to listen to his words, mournful over what had passed and describing, with little enthusiasm, the new world which he inhabited at the beginning of a new century, with all its promise, potential and uncertainty:

> There is no peace, no repose now, but there is hullabaloo, this society and that society. This must be done and that must be done, until it has become, to an old fellow like me, by no means a pleasant world. I wish I could live again in those days when I saw Jory White, Tim Wheatley and Bill Sharpe, looking over the bridge for hours; at the fish working his tail.

Greenwell died on 27 January 1918, almost reaching his own century. But, we are told: 'To the very end his interest in his beloved sport of angling never failed, and at an incredible age he went fishing in an open boat on a lake and got drenched; with perfect complacency, and indeed, some pride.'

⚜ HAMSTERLEY CASTLES ⚜

Described by English Heritage as 'an enigmatic earthwork with dry stone walls of uncertain date', Hamsterley Castles, in the parish of South Bedburn, 4 miles or so from Wolsingham, is a true curiosity.

Though called 'The Castles', it is in reality a huge, dry-stone enclosure, measuring 75m by 90m, surrounding over an acre of land. It was built in the familiar style of a Roman fortification with the trademark rounded corners. A number of archaeological hypotheses have been put forward to fully explain its history and its function, although to date none has satisfactorily done so. Therefore, as to its true purpose and as to who, if anyone, actually lived there, we must remain in the world of theory. And where true knowledge is absent, legend supplants fact.

It has been suggested that it might have been a defensive refuge for the Iron Age Brigantes tribe, retreating before the relentless march of the Roman Legions. Alternatively, it could have been a Bronze Age settlement, an Iron Age village, a Roman prison, or a Dark Age fortification providing sanctuary to a scattered and undefended local population who would have fled there in the event of violent attack. Equally, however, it may only have been a secure enclosure for keeping livestock.

Archaeological excavations have been carried out but few artefacts have been recovered from the site. Some Bronze Age flints and an arrowhead perhaps, but most enigmatic of all, as Sir Timothy Eden tells us, the disarticulated arm bones of a young woman, found many years ago in a corner of the massive enclosure.

In 2007, TV's popular and much-lamented archaeology programme *Time Team* spent its customary three days at the site and the team were baffled by the lack of physical finds. They uncovered the traces of a small number of Iron Age buildings and what were possibly cattle enclosures. They revealed what seemed to be later, probably Dark Age, additions and reinforcements to the wall, at what was presumed to be a gatehouse. But as to who had actually dwelt there, nothing more could be established.

So why would a scattering of two or three Iron Age roundhouses and a few cattle pens require such massive protection? The immense walls contained, it was calculated, over 6,000 tons of stone and had originally stood at over 11ft high and 15–20ft thick. Surely such an enclosure must have been built either to keep something in or, more likely perhaps, to keep something out. Experts agree that, although the enclosure was built in the Roman style, it was not built with Roman know-how. It is thought that whoever ordered its construction must have seen a Roman fortification, or have been familiar with one, but had neither the technology nor the skills to replicate one.

Could it then have been the military stronghold of some local warlord? A fortified bolt-hole, during the uncertain years following the withdrawal of the Roman Legions from Britain, before the advance of the Anglo-Saxons? Was this individual someone who perhaps had lived or had been garrisoned at Binchester, the Roman fort of Vinovia just a few short miles away?

Perhaps, in the end, the bones of the unknown young woman found in the enclosure serve as a metaphor for 'The Castles'. Who she was, the story of her life and her world, remain lost to today's generations. Experts may theorise, the rest of us may speculate, but the truth is nobody really knows! Their secrets remain secret. And Hamsterley Castles remains, for the time being, and perhaps for all time, both a curiosity and a mystery.

⚜ HEOROT'S LEGENDARY HALL ⚜

It is said that there has been a settlement in the vicinity of Hart Village, near Hartlepool, since well before the Norman Conquest, the area thereabouts then being known as Heortnesse. And, curiously, Hart has been proposed as the historical (if perhaps unlikely) site of Heorot, the Mead Hall of Hrothgar, Chief of the Scyldings, as described in the oldest Anglo-Saxon poem in existence: *Beowulf*.

The themes in the poem are Scandinavian in origin and it has been assumed that the tale was probably first told in sixth-century Denmark. It was then passed down orally through subsequent generations before being brought across the sea by Anglian settlers and finally being written down by an unknown writer, early in the eleventh century, at an unknown location somewhere in Anglo-Saxon England.

However, there have been those who have disputed this generally accepted theory. Daniel Henry Haigh, noted Victorian scholar of Anglo-Saxon history and author of the 1861 text *The Anglo-Saxon Sagas*, championed the idea that Hart (originally Heort) was in fact the Heorot of legend and that the landscape around it was the actual inspiration for the story's setting. The writer, he claimed, had been an unknown Northumbrian poet.

To support his theory, Haigh identified certain clues in the poem including 'peculiarities of dialect' in the text and certain local 'topographical identifications' which seemed to fit with descriptions and motifs in the story. The mere, where lurked the monster Grendel, Haigh proposed as the formerly large (and allegedly sinister) nearby pool named Bottomless Car, while the hill stream of the saga was perhaps, he suggested, inspired by the How Beck, which formerly flowed from the pool. Haigh was well aware of the dark reputation of Bottomless Car, now long since dried up. It was said to be so evil that 'the Hart chased by hounds will sooner die on the bank than plunge into that water'; a fitting lair indeed for a dreadful monster.

Haigh went further, identifying, so he asserted, other geographical locations with scenes in the poem. Of the cliff over which Beowulf's companions disposed of the monster's carcass, he said: 'The scene was evidently well known to the poet and I have no hesitation in identifying it with Eagles-Cliffe, a promontory in Durham, about fifty feet high, nearly surrounded by the Tees.'

Haigh's controversial theory was given more credence when W.H.D. Longstaffe, writing in the *Transactions of the Northumberland and Durham Archaeological Society*, seemingly corroborated the idea that other nearby place names could also be identified as locations described in the story.

Modern Anglo-Saxon scholars, however, have been less than enthusiastic about the historical effusions of Daniel H. Haigh and it has been observed, rather prosaically, that 'the identification has not been generally accepted'.

⚜ INTERMENT ⚜

Funerals are deeply personal occasions: relatives and friends either carrying out the specific last wishes of the deceased or simply demonstrating the love and respect felt by those who are left to mourn for those who have gone. Generally, however, they follow a traditional format, reflecting to a greater or lesser degree the religious or spiritual beliefs of the deceased.

The curious funeral arrangements demanded by some of our County Durham forebears would today, therefore, seem to be eccentric in the extreme.

The tradition of the deceased going to their rest in a coffin is of course well established and apparently universal; common, surely, throughout history. Well, perhaps not! It is recorded that in 1614, money was spent at St Oswald's church in Durham City, on 'makinge the coffins for to bringe the dead corpses to the church in'. A curious record no doubt, but it was usual practice at the time to bury bodies without a coffin. There may well have been a religious justification for burial without a coffin and certainly the burial service includes the words, 'When the earth shall be cast upon the body', suggesting that the deceased would be interred just as they were. A second reason may well be that coffins were expensive and therefore usually available only to those who could afford them. For everyone else, the wardens kept the parish coffin in which the dearly departed was carried to the church and grave; there to be removed and buried coffin-less.

Of equal, if not greater importance than the burial of the body, was the belief of the deceased, to whatever degree, in their own resurrection and how, on the Day of Judgement, this would be physically accomplished. There are many odd stories in connection with this notion from all across the country.

The year 1793 saw the death of John Oliver, a Sussex miller and notorious character, who, during his life, had also been suspected of being the accomplice of smugglers. He requested that his body be buried upside down because he was convinced that on Judgement Day the earth would turn topsy-turvy and he would therefore be the only one facing the right way up. This particular story is probably apocryphal but, at Box Hill in Surrey, one Major Peter Labelliere was, at his own request, actually buried head downwards.

In County Durham, we are told by E. Mackenzie and M. Ross, writing in 1834, that a certain Revd Arthur Shepherd of Pittington, who died in 1770: 'though a worthy character, entertained very singular ideas on several subjects, particularly those connected with his future state of his existence.' Just what to expect, perhaps, from a man of the cloth. However, Revd Shepherd's dying wish was apparently for a hatchet to be deposited with him, in his coffin, and for a mirror to be fixed under the coffin lid, opposite his face; both we are told: 'with a view to facilitate his resurrection.'

Another curiosity was uncovered at the beginning of the nineteenth century by workmen excavating for a new road across the moors, between Weardale and Teesdale. Allegedly they found a body, buried upright. It was believed locally to be the remains of a traveller who had disappeared many years earlier and had been thought murdered. It is unlikely, therefore, that the unusual manner of burial in this case would have been the unfortunate victim's personal choice of interment.

Unusual funeral instructions were also given by certain gentlemen who, in death, wished to share their grave with their favourite companion in life; usually their horse. A tale is told of Captain Hutton of Houghton Hall, Houghton-le-Spring, who died on 6 August 1680. Captain Hutton held decidedly Puritan beliefs and had fought with the Parliamentarian army during the English Civil War. Described as a 'bluff weather beaten soldier with coal black hair, not cropped like a roundhead, but flowing over his armour', he had requested permission from the rector of Houghton-le-Spring to bury his favourite horse in the churchyard, next to the spot he had already chosen for himself. The rector

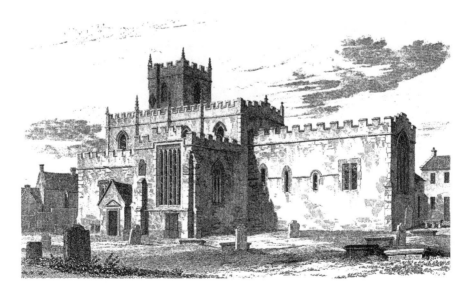

St Oswald's church, Durham City.

refused, the two men quarrelled and Captain Hutton buried the horse in his own orchard, stipulating that when he died he was to be buried alongside it. His wishes were carried out.

Burial in an orchard seems to have been the choice of many. In 1663, the Archdeacon of Durham complained that three children of Mr Massock of Headlam had been buried in an orchard without any service. And in 1684, a Mr Richardson of Caterhouse, near Durham, dying under sentence of excommunication (pronounced by Bishop Crewe), was eventually laid to rest in his own orchard.

Perhaps even more extreme were the funeral wishes expressed by William Ettrick the Sunderland magistrate. An eccentric fellow, Justice Ettrick presided for many years over his Bench. Once, after fining a local farmer for being in breach of the law by not having his name clearly visible on his cart (a cart which he used for transporting dung), the aggrieved farmer left the court to see an employee of Ettrick's driving the magistrate's own fully laden dung cart back to his farm. The cart, however, did not display Ettrick's name. The farmer immediately returned to the court and accused the magistrate of the same crime for which he'd shortly before suffered punishment. Ettrick duy put himself on trial and after considering all the evidence against him, found himself guilty and punished himself in accordance with the law.

In his Last Will and Testament, written in September 1802, Justice Ettrick set out his curious funeral wishes. He requested that: 'my body be buried at or around the hour of twelve o'clock at night; and that it may be carried in my dung cart to the grave.' He left strict instructions that his coffin had to be made of oak, 1½ inches thick; without any adornment or linings and no plate giving his name, age or date of his death. Four paupers were to lower him into the grave and there was to be no mourning of any kind at the funeral.

Justice Ettrick eventually died on 22 February 1808, at 83 years of age. His coffin was indeed made of 1½ inch oak but it had a brass plate upon the lid, properly engraved, and he was buried at Bishopwearmouth church 'at the usual hour for interments'. So much for the wishes of Justice Ettrick!

Of course, none of this would have done for Mrs Drage and a dung cart most certainly would have played no part at all in her rather grand funeral obsequies.

On 29 May 1740, the recently deceased Mrs Drage, the late wife of Theodore Drage of Bishop Auckland, was carried in her funeral procession around her home town, before her eventual interment at York. John Sykes tells us in his *Local Records*, published in 1824, that: 'As the procession was rather uncommon, it may not be uninteresting.' It is described here, as it was by Sykes:

> The deceased was dressed in her wedding suit, with a pair of new slippers on and put into
> a leaden coffin, which was inclosed in another of deal or fir; and another of fine wainscot

(brought from London) contained the other two. On the above day, the procession began in the following order; two men on horseback, in black, with caps and favours, two kettle drums in mourning; a horse led by a man on foot; two trumpeters, the trumpets hung with rich gilt escutcheons of silk; a man on horseback displaying a very large gilt escutcheon on a black pole; two singing men from the choir at Durham; two men in black cloaks, caps and favours, bearing each a pole covered with black silk.

Then followed:

The hearse, drawn by six horses, three men on horseback on each side, in black, with caps and favours; two men behind after the same manner; the Undertaker (Mr Watson, from Durham); the mourning coach drawn by six horses, in which were Mr Drage, his daughter, and two friends; and lastly, two men on horseback, in black, with caps and favours. The procession passed very slowly through all the streets of Bishop Auckland, during which time the trumpets sounded, and the drums beat in solemn manner.

But perhaps a lasting indication of the character in life of one who has passed on could best be recorded in prose, or more likely in verse, as an epitaph carved on their gravestone. The following may serve as a limited example.

Barnabas Hutchinson died in Durham on 18 March 1834; his epitaph read as follows:

Under this Thorn Tree
Lies honest Barnabee;
But where he is gone,
To Heaven or Hell,
I freely do own,
That I cannot tell.

Robert Trollop came from a family of stonemasons. He is said to have been the builder of Gateshead church and his burial in its churchyard there is referred to in his epitaph:

Here lies Robert Trollop,
Who made yon stones roll up;
When death took his soul up,
His body filled this hole up.

'In Affectionate Remembrance.'

John Lively was the vicar of Kelloe and his epitaph recorded his remarkable progeny:

Here lies John Lively, Vicar of Kelloe,
He had seven daughters and never a fellow.

❖ I TOLD YOU SO! (VINDICATED!) ❖

The following curious incident occurred at the beginning of the nineteenth century.

Richard Attee, a butcher of Middleton-in-Teesdale, held very strong opinions about the quality and strength of the bridge that was being built nearby to span the River Tees. He had, after all, a keen interest in it as he regularly had cause to cross over into Yorkshire in order to go about his business.

The bridge was being built badly, he claimed; it was unsafe, undoubtedly dangerous and he confidently – and unceasingly – predicted to anyone who would listen that it was sure to collapse, be swept away, or suffer some similar doom. Indeed, so repetitive and tiresome were his predictions on the subject that eventually they were just accepted by the villagers and ignored. Everyone was well aware that it was their butcher's 'favourite theme' but nobody took any real notice of it; the building work continued and the bridge gradually took shape.

But Attee was undaunted and his assessment remained unchanged, as did the opinions of the long-suffering villagers. That is until one day, when Attee finally persuaded some of them to go with him to view the partially built edifice. He would show them at first hand the faults in its construction that he alone had observed, finally convincing everyone, so he thought, both of the unquestionable accuracy of his predictions and of the inevitable fate of the bridge.

Once at the scene, Attee straight away and unhesitatingly ventured underneath the structure in order to point out to the assembled onlookers its serious deficiencies. As he did so, the bridge suddenly shook. Instinctively, Attee's wife rushed forward to retrieve him from any potential danger. At that very moment, to the astonishment and horror of the villagers, the bridge collapsed, just as their garrulous butcher had for so long predicted it would. Crumbling masonry crashed down and both Attee and his wife were killed.

An entry referring to Middleton, in the second volume of Mackenzie and Ross's *A Historical, Topographical and Descriptive View of the County Palatine of Durham* published in 1834, states the following: 'A handsome stone bridge of one arch, eighty feet in span, was erected across the river, about twenty years ago, by public subscription ... A previous bridge, built in 1811, fell when nearly completed.'

❧ JEMMY, THE DUKE'S PIPER ❧

James Allan was born in Northumberland in March 1734. His mother was of Gypsy stock, while his father, Will Allan, was 'a noted vermin catcher' and performer on the Northumbrian pipes. James was a man of high renown in certain circles. A brilliant exponent of the same Northumbrian pipes, he both played and composed music for the instrument, was credited with making improvements to its design, and was known the county round (familiarly if slightly inaccurately), as Jemmy, the Duke's Piper. Such was his skill that, during the years 1746 and 1747, he was engaged to play privately for the Countess of Northumberland and he was undoubtedly 'very highly regarded by his musical contemporaries'.

Unfortunately, James Allan, alternatively known as Jamie, Jimmy or Jemmy, was a man of low repute in certain other circles. He was in fact a bit of a villain, a ne'er-do-well, with a penchant for petty crime, drinking, gambling and womanising; all in all, a larger-than-life character. However, because of his musical ability, he retained the favour of the countess. We are told that he even accompanied her, in 1761, to the coronation of King George III, where the countess presented him with a set of silver and ivory pipes for the occasion and he played at the Royal Court. But, in James' case, old habits died hard and nine years later he was dismissed from service at Alnwick Castle in disgrace. Reproved for 'irregular conduct', presumably thieving, he left the castle and began a 'most extraordinary career of adventure and vagrancy'.

It was a career that began in Northumberland and County Durham and eventually even spawned two 'rather fanciful' biographies. Written after his death, James is portrayed as a likeable rogue who has countless adventures, through which he negotiates his way, with derring-do and quick-wittedness. He goes off to travel the world, seeing India, the Dutch East Indies and the Baltic. He witnesses murder, escapes from prison (and also from the French) and has amorous liaisons with numerous women.

James did indeed become a soldier on more than one occasion. He would, perhaps when he saw the opportunity to make some money, or the convenience (or necessity) of disappearing for a while, join up, stay in service for a short time and then desert. This he seems to have done repeatedly 'until he became a practised hand at the process.' Throughout his life James remained an inveterate livestock rustler and he 'varied his performances between sheep and horse stealing.' A constant 'refugee from justice', he was twice tried for felonies and twice acquitted. And all the time, he subsidised his nefarious activities by playing his pipes.

So it was that James got away with his life of shady adventuring and flights from the law and became the stuff of popular myth to the people of County Durham and Northumberland. This would all come to an end, however, in the year 1803. James had reached the ripe old age of 69 when he was convicted at the Durham Assizes of horse theft, which was then a capital offence. He had stolen a horse in Gateshead and ridden north, eventually being arrested in Jedburgh. At trial, James was sentenced to death and incarcerated, awaiting execution, in Durham's House of Correction: the dreaded Bridewell.

However, in a way, fate smiled again on James Allan; his death sentence was commuted and the old rogue escaped the hangman's rope on condition that he would await transportation to Botany Bay. Perhaps, despite his long life of petty crime and mischief, James still had influential friends, because his deportation similarly never actually took place and instead he remained condemned to a miserable, caged existence for the rest of his days. Eventually, after seven years' incarceration, with just his pipes for company and no doubt the haunting strains of many a lament echoing around the dripping stone walls of his prison, his health began to fail. James was 'afflicted with a complication of disorders'; he had come to the lowest ebb of his life in the misery and squalor of the Bridewell. It must have seemed a long time indeed since that day he had played the merry pipes at the king's coronation.

Nevertheless, even now it seemed that James was not without support. For early in 1810, a petition was raised, pleading for a Royal Pardon for the old villain and it was sent to the king in the February of that year. Fate, however, would have it that whilst a hopeful James waited for his fate to be decreed, King George III, at whose coronation James had played his pipes, had lapsed into one of his lengthy bouts of madness. Eventually a Royal Pardon was signed by the Prince Regent, acting in the

Jemmy, the duke's piper.

name of his incapacitated father. The document confirming James' fate arrived in Durham on 17 November 1810, curiously bearing the first signature of the Prince Regent officially addressed to the City of Durham. The Pardon would never reach its recipient, however, since 'death had removed him beyond the reach of Royal clemency', for James had died just four days before, aged 77.

But James Allan left behind two things. Despite his legendary, lifelong liaisons with women, he left a widow, Tibby, who eventually died at Rothbury, on 27 March 1830, aged 109 years. He also left, so it is said, a lasting echo of his presence in the old Bridewell. Indeed, where that grim place once was, there is now a bar, bearing James' name. It has been said that when the customers are gone and the place is quiet, the distant echoes of James' ghostly pipes can still be heard.

There are some aspects of James' romanticised life that are 'almost popular entertainment'; resonant of the mainly embroidered and largely false stories that built up around another horse thief, Dick Turpin, who in reality was a decidedly unromantic character. Whilst James' story is not in the same legendary league as Turpin's, a similar mythology was built up about it, and though James was a thief and a piper of some repute, to the best of this author's knowledge, he was never a murderer.

❧ JOE PIKER'S SECRET ❧

In 1822 there was a disappearance.

A young farmhand, preparing to drive sheep from Berwick-upon-Tweed to market in Newcastle, had a violent quarrel with his lover. It was afterwards assumed that, in his anger, he had killed her and disposed of her body before vanishing to escape the retribution of the law. None of this was known for certain, but the quarrelling lovers were never seen again in Berwick and their family and friends were left to assume the worst.

Josiah Charles Stephenson lived at Toft Hill, near Bishop Auckland. Known to the villagers as Joe Piker because his cottage stood next to a turnpike gate, he had come to the area as a young man and lived amongst his neighbours for nearly fifty years.

Originally his lifestyle had been a solitary one; keeping himself to himself and making no real friends, he had survived on the parish dole. Eventually, however, he had courted and won the hand of Sally, a serving girl at the The Bull, and, in order to keep food on their table and a roof over their heads, Joe secured regular Datal work (casual labour secured on a daily basis). In the winter he would hew coal at one of the local pits and in the summer he would secure employment at the nearby farms, showing considerable aptitude for the work. And so, although they were never blessed with children, for thirty years Joe and Sally lived a quiet, happy life until the sad day when Sally passed away.

Joe was distraught and vowed that never again would he marry. How could Sally be replaced? A couple of years later, however, he did remarry. But the collective eyebrows of the villagers were well and truly raised. Joe's choice of bride was not a popular one with his neighbours; the woman in question was generally disliked, shunned even. She, so they thought, was a gossip and a troublemaker and no fit replacement for the ever-loyal Sally. Sure enough, it seemed that Joe's hopes of finding again the happiness that he'd had with his beloved first wife had been misplaced. After less than two weeks, his new bride left him.

Straight away she gave full vent to her poisonous gossiping tongue. Joe Piker, she claimed, had a shocking secret; something that he had kept hidden from everyone. But the woman's vindictive nature went before her: she was ignored and eventually 'jeered out of the place for her inventions' and for her cruelty to the unfortunate Joe.

But the truth of it was, Joe had always been a bit of a loner; his origins a bit of a mystery. And this unfortunate episode brought about a marked change in both his personality and his life. Over the course of the next few years, he increasingly mistrusted and shunned company, especially and perhaps unsurprisingly the company of women, whom he would not even suffer inside the 'miserable hovel' in which he eventually became 'a solitary and decrepit recluse'. He had never been a very pious man but as time marched on, year after dreary year, the increasingly sad figure of Joe Piker 'rapidly developed into a most blasphemous old reprobate, whose profanity, excited by the most trivial annoyances, was truly blood-curdling'.

Joe's became a miserable existence. Once, after a rare few drinks with a crony, he let slip that his childhood home had been Berwick-upon-Tweed. His companion, out of sympathy for Joe's condition, suggested that he may want to return there and even offered to try and contact any surviving family and friends Joe might have; the kind offer was vehemently refused. There were also times when Joe's clouded eyes would seemingly drift away to view once more scenes either far distant or long ago and he would mutter vaguely and enigmatically about how, following his death, there would be a sensation in the village such as there had never been before.

Towards the end of 1869, Joe took ill and it was clear that the end of his life was approaching. A kindly female neighbour offered to help him but the offer was greeted with the same mistrust and disdain as was usual and Joe continued in solitude until, eventually, he did indeed die. Soon after, two old women from the village entered his 'miserable hovel' to attend to the traditional offices for the deceased and the preparation of his body for burial. They were quickly followed by the village doctor, then, unusually, and causing great consternation and excitement throughout the village, by the constable. Whatever Joe Piker's dark secret had been it was, it seemed, finally uncovered. And the secret was? That Joe Piker, who had lived among them for some forty years, was in fact a woman.

Enquiries about Joe's background were made, as far as possible, by the local vicar. All that could definitely be established though was that Joe had first reached Toft Hill in 1823. It was already know that *he* had hailed from Berwick-upon-Tweed and, the story of the lovers' quarrel there in 1822 being widely told, it was assumed that Joe had actually been the young girl who had been spurned by the farmhand. It was believed that in a fit of rage the girl had killed her 'faithless lover' before disposing of his body, taking his clothes and assuming the identity of a male. Unable to remain in the town, she had journeyed south to County Durham, eventually beginning a new life in Toft Hill.

Joe Piker's burial was recorded in the parish church register at Etherley. It said simply and rather sadly: 'An unknown woman: died 23 November, 1869.'

❖ KETTON'S COLOSSUS ❖

Today I suppose we think of the phrase 'National Tour' mainly in relation to some form of entertainment: music perhaps, the latest pop sensation or a travelling opera, a West End hit show or ballet company or sometimes a popular comedian. We do not necessarily think of a 220-stone Shorthorn bull. But at the beginning of the nineteenth century, this really was the headline act and it made a very healthy living for Mr John Day, the owner of the famous beast which would become known as 'The Durham Ox'.

Around this time there had been an explosion of interest in local agricultural shows, especially in the competitions which offered cash prizes for the best stock animals. So it was that in 1796, Charles Colling Jnr of Ketton bred, from one of his improved Durham Shorthorn bulls and 'a common black and white cow, bought for £14 at Durham Market', the calf that would eventually become the famous 'Ketton Ox' (later renamed the 'Durham Ox'). Colling even commissioned a painting of it and the young, 168-stone animal would become the star attraction at Darlington Market.

In 1801, Colling sold his prize beast for £140 to a Mr Bulmer, a Yorkshire man who intended to exhibit the Ketton Ox for money. Bulmer had a special carriage made to transport his exhibit, no small consideration for an animal so large. Clearly, however, such an undertaking would face serious problems, not least in view of the dreadful state of the public highways of the day. After just five weeks and 197 miles, Bulmer gave up on his moneymaking idea and sold both the ox and the carriage for £250.

They were purchased by John Day and his plan was much the same; to travel to various locations and invite the public to view the magnificent animal for the price of admission. Within twenty-four hours, he had started touring. The young beast was now nearly 6 years old, weighed 171 stone and was still growing. But Day proved to be tirelessly ambitious, well organised and very promotionally savvy. His knack for publicity soon paid off. Shortly after he'd bought the ox, he was offered 500 guineas for it; a few months later, in June 1801, he received an offer (which he refused) of £2,000; clearly, a serious amount of money at the time.

It was now that the animal was rebranded as the Durham Ox. It would become 'the most famous of the notable individual beasts which achieved prominence in England at the beginning of the nineteenth century', and the career of Mr John Day and his travelling attraction was well under way. In 1802, he commissioned a new portrait of the ox and had copies made, for sale to an adoring public. In the year after its release, 2,000 were sold: 'from whence the public opinion of this beautiful animal may well be ascertained.' Renowned, the ox may have been an exemplar of its breed, but it was John Day who turned it into a true star.

The specially designed carriage had to be pulled across the country by six or sometimes eight horses, depending on the condition of the roads. Day himself would ride with the team while his wife, apparently long suffering, would travel in the carriage itself with the ox, which continued to put on weight, eventually passing 216 stone. Luckily for her it seemed to possess a temperament suited to touring, for although Day tells us that when not confined to the carriage it was 'vigorous and extremely active', sometimes 'leaping over a water trough, two feet high, with as much activity and frolic as a one-year-old', it was also docile: '[he] became so domesticated that my wife, who rode with him in the carriage, found him harmless as a fawn, and familiar as a lap dog.'

For six years, between 1801 and 1807, John Day toured virtually non-stop with his attraction. They criss-crossed the country from east to west and travelled the long miles from London and the Home Counties into the south and up to Scotland, visiting 200 different locations in all. The fame of the Durham Ox went before it and the money kept rolling in.

Then, sadly, early in 1807, when about 10 years old, the ox reached Oxford and accidentally dislocated a hip. Day did all he could to have the problem rectified but to no avail. The only option left was to have it destroyed and Sykes tells us, in his *Local Records*, that at its death, the enormous beast weighed 220 stone. After the grisly deed had been done (and with a startling lack of sentiment about the animal that had, for seven years, been his constant companion, and main source of income), Day listed with some pride the weight of each individual portion of the slaughtered beast, divided up by the butchers, and said of its meat that it was: 'the best in every way.'

The fame of the Durham Ox lived on long after its physical demise. It was not the largest or the heaviest of beasts ever exhibited, for others both larger and heavier would come after. But we are told that it was an 'extremely large, exceptionally handsome animal' with 'fine proportion and perfect symmetry of form' and a 'fine, smooth coat of red mixed with white'.

In the journals of the farming fraternity, the Durham Ox would often be written about, and its picture reproduced. In academic works concerned with livestock selection and breeding, it would be held up as an exemplar and model of its kind. Publicly, many ale houses, inns and coffee shops were named, or indeed changed their name to the Durham Ox. Paintings, woodcuts and engravings also followed and twenty years after it was eaten, a series of blue and white tableware pieces were produced, upon which were shown images of the colossal beast, set against artistically appropriate rustic scenes.

Of John Day, nothing more is heard after 1807, but he did write a thirty-two-page account of his life and travels with the Durham Ox, a copy of which survives, bizarrely perhaps, in the library of Yale University, in the USA. Day's account was, in his own words, 'A most valuable record of the life of the Durham Ox, during those years in which its lasting fame was established.'

❧ KIDDING OR WHAT! – OR NOT? ❧

When we think of large, hairy bipedal hominids (if we think of them at all) we usually associate those two cryptozoological exemplars of the type, the yeti and the sasquatch (or Bigfoot), with wild and reassuringly distant places; the dizzying remoteness of the Himalayan Mountain range or the vast, dense forests of Canada and north-western USA. Creatures such as these, if they exist at all, surely have no place in twenty-first century Britain, or indeed in County Durham. Well, perhaps not!

But we do have our own tales to tell! Stories persist of strange and alarming encounters in the UK, with terrifying tales of the Fear Liath Mor (the Big Grey Man) of Ben MacDhui in Scotland's Cairngorm Mountains. These encounters are not, in the main, with something visible, but with something hidden, something fearful. Seemingly veiled from human eyesight, it gives away its presence and instils its terror with audible and seemingly pursuing footsteps. Footsteps made, so witnesses report, by something huge, unseen and which almost always exudes a feeling of disturbing malevolence. Perhaps these experiences are not real in the true sense, but are simply the external manifestations of sudden, unexplained and irrational feelings of dread or threat. Terror, brought about by the psychological effect of an often perceived feeling of isolation and otherworldliness, in a high, wild place.

Away from the mountains there are other strange tales; tales of the forests and legends harking back to stories familiar in folklore, of the woodwose of mythology: the 'Wild Man of the Woods'. It is thought that these legends were brought to our shores by Dark Age settlers and the creatures described in them were no more than that: legends and fairy tales. Passing generations have continued to depict them as shadowy, illusive, legendary denizens of the deep, dark forest, but is that really all that they are?

There have been numerous modern-day reports of terrifying encounters with mysterious creatures in the woods. Over the past thirty years, alarming incidents have occurred from Devon to Dunbartonshire, from Somerset to Staffordshire and from Derbyshire to Yorkshire. Many details of the alleged sightings share striking similarities. Witnesses report encounters with bipedal creatures described invariably as man-like or ape-like, covered in brown or black hair and standing anything up to 3m tall. They have been encountered in daylight and during the hours of darkness. They have been sighted by a variety of witnesses, including individuals, groups of walkers, families, holidaymakers and even motorists. Sometimes the onlooker describes the sighting of the creature as a mere glimpse, before it slips away into the forest. On other occasions, it is seen, seemingly observing the witness, peering out from the woodland cover. There have also been, perhaps more alarmingly, occasions when the creature seemed to follow from a distance, as if stalking its prey. The impression is normally of a flesh and blood creature, exhibiting animal-like behaviour perhaps much like the woodwose of legend. Such reports are curious enough but there are other, far weirder stories of, well, *something* else.

A number of alarming reports tell of something quite different; something large, black and bipedal but this time with the sinister addition of baleful, glowing red eyes. These strange sightings have not been restricted to the deep woods but have occurred at a number of random locations, from the banks of a reservoir or a lake to the roadside verge, or a lane leading from a pub to the main road. They have been witnessed from Sherwood Forest to Dundonald Castle in Ayrshire; from Cannock Chase to Royal Tunbridge Wells. They have also been witnessed in Northumberland and, also, in County Durham.

These reports tend to differ from those previously mentioned, as witnesses attest to the out-and-out weirdness of their experience. Whatever it is that is seen does not fall easily into the category of some kind of animal and does not, on the whole, behave naturally. Witnesses sometimes also describe an overwhelming feeling of dread, both during and after the sighting, and a sense that what they witnessed did not appeal to the instinct as something of flesh and blood but somehow *something else*; not a creature as such, but some other form of entity.

The Beast of Bolam made news during the winter of 2002/03, being witnessed in woodland adjacent to Bolam Lake, in Northumberland. There had been whispers of strange sightings at the site over the previous five years but things came to a head when a mother and child, crossing the car park, were terrified by a huge, black, man-shaped creature, standing motionless amongst the trees. A group of anglers were confronted at night by a similar figure, with glowing red eyes, which, according to measurements later taken at the site, must have stood around 8ft tall. Other witnesses came forward and these curious incidents were widely reported in the press and on TV. All the witnesses appeared to be convinced that what they had seen was real, but no physical evidence for it was ever found and subsequent investigations, including one by the Centre for Fortean Zoology, could offer no explanation for the sightings of the so-called Geordie Bigfoot.

Six years later, reports appeared on the Internet about the following incident. On 10 October 2009, a couple had enjoyed an evening out at a public house near Seaham, County Durham. At about 10 p.m., they left to walk the short distance down a lane to the main road. What they claimed to have seen during this short walk terrified them. As they glanced up, there, slightly in front of them, in a field on the other side of the hedge, they witnessed a huge, man-shaped figure standing black in the surrounding darkness. They estimated its height at about 7ft and its glowing red eyes seemed to be staring straight at them. They stood rooted to the spot, speechless. After a short time, the figure uttered a piercing, high-pitched cry and promptly disappeared down behind the hedge 'as if dropping through a trap door'. Not wishing, perhaps understandably, to investigate further, the unfortunate couple ran off without looking back. Once again an investigation followed. Once again the incident remained unexplained. So here, it seems, we are in the realm of the very curious indeed.

Various theories have been put forward. In some cases it is suggested that such sightings could be escapees from zoos or possibly from private collections: if it looks like a monkey and it behaves like a monkey, then it's probably a monkey! Others suggest that sightings are simply optical illusions or tricks on the eye played by light or shadow which cause the brain to respond by forming substance where no substance exists.

Of course there are those who would have us believe that these creatures are real. Not, perhaps, in a physical sense, but as liminal beings existing at the very edges of our world or our consciousness. Further to this, they are even described as interdimensional creatures which appear in but do not exist in our world or our reality, much in the same way as the 1966/67 Mothman phenomenon of Point Pleasant, West Virginia, USA. Charles Hoy Fort, that well-known American collector of the curious, suggested that 'they fade in and out of this time and dimension through some accident of Metaphysics'. Others, however, would assert that these entities are ghostly in nature, appearing suddenly to the unsuspecting and the unprepared, for reasons known only to themselves.

There may well be more stories of such strange encounters, as yet unknown to the general public, simply because witnesses are reluctant to report them for fear of ridicule. Of course, many people would simply say of the sightings that they're all just hoaxes, someone kidding us, having a laugh. Such bizarre accounts make for a good story, but in the end they aren't much more than that.

Then again, many of us go for walks over hills, along field margins and riverbanks and, of course, through woods. Yet in our gentle, unadventurous perambulations, how many of us stray from the path? As if guided and protected by some common memory, we tend not to stray from the way through the woods. After all, we don't know what might be lying in wait for us if we do.

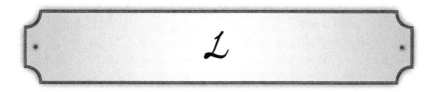

⁖ LILY OF LUMLEY ⁖

It is (probably) a truth universally acknowledged that a castle should be haunted. Any ancient fortification without its due compliment of spectral inhabitants seems somewhat incomplete. In County Durham, however, our castles seem reassuringly replete with ghostly goings-on. Some stories emanating from these ancient structures seem to belong exactly there, in the realm of story. Everyone *knows* about the ghost, but nobody can actually remember when it was last seen, or by whom. However, there are other ghost accounts which, somewhat strangely, seem to receive more attention and more coverage in the cold light of today than they ever did in the smoke-stained, candle-lit chronicles of Victorian times.

Since its first tentative steps onto the national professional cricket stage in 1991, when Durham County Cricket Club joined the senior level of the English County Championship, the Durham Cricket Team has, at the time of writing, been crowned English County Champions three times in six seasons and reached the very pinnacle of the English game. Over that time, the County Ground at the Riverside, Chester-le-Street, has played host to some of the world's best cricketers, from both the domestic and the international game. Some of those players have stayed at Lumley Castle, now the renowned hotel, which seems to stand sentry, a lone outfielder, overlooking the cricket ground itself.

There has been a stronghold on that spot for centuries. A manor house belonging to the Lumley family stood there in ancient times and, around 1398, that manor house was strengthened and fortified to become what we know today as Lumley Castle. Like most castles, its walls have seen acts of violence over the centuries and, so the theory goes, these violent events have imprinted their record into the very fabric of the castle. These impressions give rise to a well-known, and apparently well-documented, haunting which has become a staple of County Durham ghostlore. However, as with many well-known ghost stories, the addition and subtraction of various details in the telling has led to a number of variations in the tale. What follows is, no doubt, just one account of the tragic events which led to the haunting of Lumley Castle.

Sir Ralph Lumley resided at his fortress home with his wife, Lady Lily, who had become a religious adherent of John Wycliffe, the 'Morning Star of the Reformation'. Thought to have been born at the village of the same name (Wycliffe), on the south bank of the River Tees, not far from Barnard Castle, Wycliffe railed against what he saw as a corrupt and self-serving Church establishment and agitated for the Bible to be translated into English, so that all the people, and not just the priestly few, had direct access to the word of God. The Church reacted by naming him a heretic and condemned as the same anyone who followed his teachings.

The story goes that, in the absence of Sir Ralph, Lily was visited by a delegation of monks (or perhaps priests) who tried in vain to persuade her to recant her allegiance to the heretic Wycliffe. They threatened her with the damnation of her immortal soul but still she refused their demands, until at the last, whether by accident or design, the Lady Lily was killed and her body disposed of down the well, then situated in the courtyard. After hearing what had transpired, the grief-stricken Sir Ralph had the culprits arrested and put to death. However, it seems that the shades of both the sad lady and her executed assailants still return to the scene of the tragedy, to haunt Lumley Castle's darkened corridors and shadowy precincts.

In bright, sunny, June 2005, the castle (now a hotel) played host to the Australian cricket team. Curious reports began to surface that some of the players had been disturbed during the night, apparently by ghostly goings-on. The disturbances

Lumley Castle in around 1820.

were apparently so alarming that one of the Australians, Shane Watson, ended up sleeping on the floor of a teammate's bedroom. So what happened? There were whispers, unconfirmed, that the phantom of a woman had been seen during the night. One witness reputedly claimed that, on retiring, the bedroom's window blinds had been firmly closed. However, when suddenly awakened around 4 a.m., the blinds were fully open and passing by the window could be seen what looked like a procession of ghostly people. 'It was amazing,' said the witness, 'but very scary; I saw ghosts! I swear I'm telling the truth.'

Of course, the local press took a keen interest and the Australian cricket team's media officer tried to play down the incident, simply saying that: 'several of the players were uneasy, although a lot of them in the morning said they were fine.' A spokesman for the castle said, rather nonchalantly, that the Australians weren't the first to have had such an alarming experience, but if they had seen Lily, they had been lucky 'as she appears quite rarely'. The gentlemen of the press were then reminded of an incident five years before, when three members of the West Indian cricket team, including the captain, had been so scared that they had actually checked out.

No doubt a good ghost tale adds to the mystique of any building, especially a castle. But it is to be wondered if ghosts are good for business or bad. Unfortunately, no more can be gleaned about the murder or the haunting of Lumley Castle as many of the old Victorian chronicles and histories are strangely silent on the matter. It may just be a completely unfounded rumour that some visiting cricketers now prefer to avoid a stay at Lumley Castle …

⁂ LOST BOMBERS ⁂

In 1942, a curious wartime incident occurred in Durham City; an incident that would come to be added to the old city's pantheon of legends. This particular urban legend was not merely 'a story related as having actually happened', for it did actually happen, and it was witnessed by a variety of people. However, because of the mystery surrounding the night's events, its actual cause was then, and no doubt remains today, a matter of personal interpretation.

Nazi Germany's bombing campaign against Great Britain continued to spread terror amongst the civilian population. In the early hours of 1 May 1942, Durham City and its Norman cathedral were bathed in bright moonlight: a perfect target for Luftwaffe bombers. An initial warning that enemy aircraft were approaching the County Durham coast had been received at 2.33 a.m. Shortly before 3 a.m., the air-raid siren dutifully wailed its mournful warning and aircraft were heard, fast approaching the city. Almost as if in response to the coming danger, a thick, white mist suddenly and uncannily rose up from the River Wear below, engulfing both the cathedral and castle and hiding them from the bomber's view. For some time the enemy planes circled blindly overhead, before eventually simply turning away without releasing their deadly load, which soon after they dropped harmlessly at Grange Colliery and on the loop of the river at Finchale. When, at 4.02 a.m., the all-clear was sounded, the protective mist subsided and Durham City, its great cathedral and the people living within the city boundaries, were left undamaged and unharmed.

A number of individuals, mostly those on Civil Defence duties, witnessed what happened and they were later to recall their own personal and widely differing interpretations of the strange event that had taken place.

It was said by some that the mist had risen so quickly, even as the bombers were heard approaching the city, that it must have been a deliberate smokescreen triggered by the authorities to protect Durham's historic heart. Others, including the chief ARP warden on duty that night, said that though seemingly mysterious, the rising mist had merely been a natural and fairly regularly seen phenomenon, caused by the local climatic effects of night air on river water. It was simply coincidence, they maintained, that it had happened just as the Luftwaffe planes approached the city.

But there were also those who considered what had happened to be the work of a higher power. Some claimed it was a miracle and ascribed it to St Cuthbert, whose remains lay in high honour in Durham Cathedral. After all, had it not

been the case that the monkish guardians of Cuthbert's body had arrived in AD 995, after fleeing from the aggressors of their day, and in his honour had founded the ancient city? And it was Cuthbert, some were convinced, who had now protected his city from the new aggressor.

Official records confirmed that there had indeed been a large-scale Luftwaffe raid across the North East that night. Sunderland and the shipyard areas around South Shields, Jarrow and Newcastle were all extensively bombed. So the bombers heard over Durham City may have originally formed a small part of that larger raid and had simply become lost. Intriguingly, however, the incident also coincided with the latest Nazi aerial offensive against British civilians.

The view from South Street.

In the spring of 1942, RAF Bomber Command introduced a new tactic in its escalating campaign against Nazi Germany. Large formations of heavily armed bombers began to attack German towns and cities. Two of these targets were the old Hanseatic League cities of Lübeck and Rostock. During the attack, Lübeck's medieval cathedral was destroyed, while in Rostock, the ancient part of the city was obliterated. The reaction of Adolf Hitler was swift and predictable; a new Nazi offensive would be launched, aimed at British cities of historic or cultural importance.

The Baedeker travel guides carried information about many of these British cities and the deputy head of the German Foreign Office press department, the rather picturesquely named Baron Gustav Braun von Stumm, reportedly warned: 'now the Luftwaffe will go out for every building marked with three stars and more in Baedeker.' Perhaps unsurprisingly, the Luftwaffe high command did not, contrary to popular belief, use information contained in a series of travel guides to plan their bombing campaign, but both the idea and the name stuck. In April 1942, the bombs of the so-called Baedeker Blitz began to rain down and over 1,600 people would lose their lives. Exeter, Bath and Norwich had already been hit and only two nights before the Durham City incident, York had been bombed.

Was Durham to share the same fate?

A legitimate Baedeker target had to possess some or all of the following features: a major cathedral, monastic remains, a castle, city walls, medieval housing and a congested town centre. Above all, it must have a historic core, concentrated within an area small enough to be devastated by a limited attack force. Clearly Durham City fitted the criteria for a Baedeker target but has never been recognised nor even considered as one, perhaps because, in the end, no bombs ever fell.

An account of what happened in Durham City on the morning of 1 May 1942 was later published in a 1945 edition of *The Leader* magazine, in which the incident was compared to the story of the appearance of the Angels of Mons during the First World War. Personal testimonies from those who had been present that night were followed by a somewhat florid account of the events surrounding a 'Miraculous Mist', published in the *Durham County Advertiser*.

One lady, looking across to the city from the vicinity of Cassop, claimed that she witnessed the whole incident and confirmed that the mist began to rise rapidly, even as the enemy bombers could be heard approaching, transforming bright moonlight to dense fog. 'Truly,' she said, 'I saw the hand of God.' A young female member of the Royal Observer Corps, who stood on fire watch duty in South Street, directly overlooking the great western towers of the cathedral, also recounted her experience. So profound was it for her that on returning indoors after the all-clear had sounded, she recalled: 'As I closed the front door, I paused for a moment, removing my tin hat, and stood in silence; and with bowed head thanked God for our deliverance … I shall believe to the end of my days that I witnessed a miracle.'

So, modern-day miracle or modern-day myth? A fanciful account of a natural – if odd – phenomenon, or a timely demonstration of divine intervention?

Whatever the real cause of the curious incident in Durham City on the morning of 1 May 1942, for the believer, no proof is needed. Others will insist that there is always a rational explanation for that which, on occasion, defies the norm.

The argument, no doubt, goes on even to this day.

⁂ MARY BENTON, THE OLDEST WOMAN IN THE WORLD ⁂

Once upon a time, County Durham laid claim to be the home of the oldest woman in the world.

Because of her prodigious age, she was a person of much interest and was frequently visited by the curious, who would travel from great distances to hear her tales of years gone by. In return, the curious would be generous, leaving money, which perhaps afforded her a more comfortable existence.

This esteemed elderly lady was Mary Benton (*née* Lodge) who had been born, so it was stated, on 12 February 1731 in the parish of Cockfield. Her father, Ralph Lodge, had also been long lived, eventually expiring at the venerable age of 105. In her early years, Mary had lived with her grandmother, who kept an inn at Piercebridge. Later she married a butcher, John Benton, who, we are told, was 'a graceless spendthrift' and Mary eventually left him. But so it was that Mary Lodge had become Mary Benton, and that was how she would be remembered for posterity.

In her later years she lived at Elton, near Stockton-on-Tees, sharing her home with her only, aged daughter. Here she would greet visitors and tell them tales of her youth and her time at Piercebridge. Her vivid memories became tales in the telling with stories of the British Army Redcoats that were garrisoned there in 1745 during the second Jacobite Rebellion and the claiming of the British throne by Charles Edward Stuart, Bonnie Prince Charlie. Mary told of the terror the locals felt at the time, but whether from the Scottish threat or from the Redcoats is not recorded.

Curious eyes described Mary thus: 'Her form was bent, but her conversation was free and lively. Her eyes, though dimmed, were intelligent; she was able to dispense with the assistance of spectacles to the last.' She was even the subject of admiring verse, written in response to her youthful memories:

Then she graced a village scene,
When the bold Pretender came;
Can this being then have been?
Can she be the very same?

She was then a growing girl,
In King George the Second's day;
Who his banner did unfurl,
To drive the intruding Scot away.

And the soldiers quartered there,
Praised her neat and modest mien;
Her rosy cheek and raven hair,
In budding brightness then were seen.

The last eventually did come for Mary Benton and the 'Old Woman of Elton' was buried on 7 January 1853. She had lived, if her stated birth date was correct, to the venerable age of 122, though the plate on her coffin gave her age as a mere 117.

The *Guinness World Records 2013* tells us that the oldest person ever, a French lady named Jeanne Louise Calment, lived to the verified age of 122 years, 164 days. In total only four people, all women, have lived beyond 117 years. Therefore the age recorded on Mary Benton's coffin, if correct, would still make her one of the oldest women ever to have lived.

Aside from her incredible longevity, there was nothing particularly remarkable about Mary Benton. Her bold claim to be the oldest woman in the world is perhaps plausible but it must have been difficult to substantiate in the mid-nineteenth century and is certainly impossible to verify in the twenty-first.

Nonetheless, for those who saw fit for her to be remembered, it is perhaps enough that she was the oldest woman in *their* world.

❧ MASTER HUMPHREYS' CURIOUS CLOCK ❧

This is the story of a clock, two well-known works of literature and an imagined conversation.

In 1806, Thomas Humphreys began his working life apprenticed to a Mr Thwaites, a clockmaker of Barnard Castle. Six years later, Humphreys began work for another clockmaker, John Bolton, and for three years he perfected his craft in Bolton's Chester-le-Street shop. In 1815, he returned to Barnard Castle and set up in business on his own, with a sign above his shop door proudly proclaiming 'Humphreys Clockmaker'.

Eventually, Humphreys' young son, William, took his place in the family business, showing, if anything, even more skill than his father. Their reputation grew, business boomed, and Messrs Humphreys 'supplied timekeepers to all the important mansions in North Yorkshire'.

At about the age of 16, William began work on a new clock to his own design, a 'centre-second, pendulum clock, with dead beat movement'. This new clock incorporated improvements, not before introduced, to counteract the effects of variations in temperature on the pendulum. He then purchased from an acquaintance the old ornamental case of a now defunct seventeenth-century Dutch clock and installed in it his own new timepiece. His pride and joy was then 'placed in the niche, on the right hand side of the glass shop door', where passers-by and potential customers could see it and, hopefully, marvel at the skill of its creator.

In 1838 Charles Dickens came to Barnard Castle whilst researching his latest work about the infamous Yorkshire Schools which had a reputation as cheap, badly run, boys' boarding schools, where cruelty and neglect were common. He stayed at the King's Head, not far from Humphreys' premises, and as part of his daily routine, he would visit the shop to ascertain the correct time. So it was that the clock 'in the niche, on the right hand side of the glass shop door' caught the author's eye. In his book *County Durham*, Sir Timothy Eden imagines the following exchange: 'Did you make that?' asked Dickens; 'No, it was my lad there', replied Humphreys senior. 'Ah!' exclaimed the author, 'So that is Master Humphreys' Clock, is it?'

Master Humphreys' Curious Clock.

Dickens was also apparently intrigued by the other contents of Humphreys' shop, as, at the back, there was a 'miscellaneous collection of toys, various kinds of clocks, philosophical instruments; and relics'. It was indeed, thought Dickens, a veritable curiosity shop.

Partly through his association with Humphreys, Dickens managed to obtain an introduction to William Shaw, proprietor of Shaw's Academy, in nearby Bowes, typical of the kind of establishment he wished to see. Shaw was known personally to Humphreys, but when the curious party visited his academy, they were unwelcome and were quickly shown the door. It is said that Shaw never forgave Humphreys for the unwanted intrusion but, even after so short a visit, Dickens had valuable material. His novel *Nicholas Nickleby* soon followed. Shaw's Academy, it was said, became the dreaded Dotheboys Hall and some thought that

William Shaw himself was the model for the detested tyrant Wackford Squeers, though Dickens maintained that the character was a composite of a number of individuals. The book was a great success, selling 50,000 copies on the first day.

On his return from a subsequent successful lecture tour of America, Charles Dickens sent Humphreys an author copy of his novel. The package also included a letter in which Dickens said he'd had an idea for his next work which, he thought (no doubt as an acknowledgement of his association with Humphreys Clockmakers of Barnard Castle, and in recollection perhaps of the curious clock he saw 'in the niche, on the right hand side of the glass shop door'), would be entitled *Master Humphrey's Clock.*

William Humphreys eventually moved, with his famous clock, to Hartlepool, where he set up his own lifelong business, as a clockmaker, in the High Street. And the *Monthly Chronicle* tells us that: 'Nothing delighted him more, in his later days, than to describe to his friends and acquaintances, his connection with Charles Dickens, and his lengthy experience as a North Country clockmaker.' He died at Stranton, Hartlepool, on Tuesday, 24 May 1887, aged 75 and was buried in All Saint's churchyard. That same year, his old clock featured in the Newcastle Jubilee Exhibition 'when it was still keeping excellent time'.

Charles Dickens went on to become one of our greatest novelists and his visit to Barnard Castle is well known and lives on as part of our county's history. Humphreys Clockmakers' shop, however, is long gone. The building in which it was housed was pulled down in 1933 and the site, at Amen Corner, is now marked only by a commemorative plaque.

It is said that another clock used to stand on the platform of the former station at Barnard Castle and it bore the surely fitting inscription: 'This is a genuine Master Humphreys' Clock, a product of the skill of the Barnard Castle clockmakers, immortalised by Charles Dickens.'

❖ MIRACULOUS MARITIME PRESERVATIONS ❖

'For those in peril on the sea' are words familiar to many people and form probably the best-known line of the hymn 'Eternal Father, Strong to Save'.

To those who travelled across the oceans on great journeys or to those who simply made their living on the sea around our coast, danger was an occupational hazard and a constant companion.

Thomas Hutchinson hailed from Stockton-on-Tees. A married man with young children, he owned a small skiff in which he 'took in white sand from the bed of the River Tees'. On the afternoon of 23 January 1795, whilst plying his trade, he was blown out to sea by the sudden, vicious, south-westerly winds of a violent storm. Soon he was out of sight of land, his small boat floundering helplessly. Day turned to night and still the storm raged, setting him further and further adrift:

> With fainting voice I call assistance,
> Call, but there is none to hear;
> Every help is at a distance,
> My drooping soul's appall'd with fear,
> All around my eye-balls flashing
> Seek some distant mountain's brow,
> Nought I hear but torrents dashing,
> Nought but Heav'n can save me now.

Night came, but when it did it was a night curiously without darkness, as the white surf on the breaking swell gave him just light enough to bale water from his slowly sinking boat. All through the night the tempest raged and the exhausted Hutchinson, his body aching, continued frantically to bale: 'his severe labour, the probable means of his preservation, was the constant and sole object of his attention.' The next day dawned but without any sight of land. Lost, blown and drifting with vision of only a few yards, all hope began to leave him:

> See! My boat with water filling
> Soon must sink beneath the wave!
> The dreadful thought my fancy chilling
> Lends my arm the strength to lave,
> A little lighten'd by my labour,
> Hope revives within my breast,
> Hope, a kind and friendly neighbour,
> Soothes the mourning soul to rest.

January daylight soon faded to darkness. A dreadful day began to give way to the prospect of a fearful and probably fateful night:

> Dreadful still is all around me
> No glimpse of cheerful shore is nigh
> Death in hideous forms surrounds me
> Hear, oh hear my earnest cry!
> Alone, exhausted, tempest-driv'n
> Here my labours all must end
> Protect my wife, all righteous Heav'n
> And be to my poor babes a friend!

Then suddenly, and cruelty of cruelties, a large ship loomed out of the darkness on a heading straight toward him. It seemed that it was about to run him down! Had he had laboured in vain to keep his little boat afloat and his own soul from the clutches of the deep, only to be smashed to pieces by another vessel? Miraculously, he was spotted and rescued by the ship, *Argo*, which had set sail from Sunderland and had been caught in the same storm. Taken up and standing in relief on the rolling deck he witnessed 'what renders this providential escape more wonderful'. Within ten minutes of being rescued, his own little boat, that had carried him to safety for more than twenty-four hours, was smashed by a wave and sunk:

> And I can see without emotion
> While on this safe deck I tread
> My little boat sink in the ocean
> Through various perils hither led
> 'Tis gone and ye who hear my story
> Join in praise to Heav'n above
> To HIM alone be pow'r and glory
> To us benevolence and love.

When the rescue took place, the nearest land to *Argo* and to Hutchinson was the Holy Island of Lindisfarne, off the Northumberland coast.

A poem of eleven verses, from which the above descriptive lines of Hutchinson's peril and 'miraculous preservation' are taken, appeared in the *Gentleman's Magazine* in March 1796. The poem was written by Hutchinson himself.

Another curious maritime incident is recorded by Mackenzie and Ross. This incident took place early in the eighteenth century and concerned an experienced sea captain also, curiously, from Stockton known simply as 'Old Cockerell'.

Cockerell, it seems, was caught in a violent night time storm at sea, the dangerous situation quickly becoming grave as the darkness closed in, the wind howled and the ship rolled wildly and blindly as the huge swell swept the decks. The old captain began to say silent prayers for his own deliverance. Suddenly a huge wave loomed over him and tons of water crashed like a giant hammer blow across the ship, engulfing everything. Cockerell, caught in its pitiless embrace, was carried overboard and down into the boiling blackness below.

Accepting the fate that now seemed inevitable and expecting soon to meet his maker, Cockerell was lifted up from his certain doom by another wave, immense in size, which swept back across his vessel, depositing him safely back on the deck. The storm eventually blew itself out, the wind died down and the waves subsided: Old Cockerell had survived. We are told that the old man marked

The Durham coast at Hartlepool in around 1829.

the remembrance of, and thanksgiving for, his seemingly miraculous escape by: 'Never afterwards suffering his beard to be shaved, and keeping the day of the week on which it happened (it was a Wednesday), a solemn fast.'

Martin Douglas, born in Sunderland on 23 November 1777, had a quite different, but nonetheless equally curious experience. When he was aged only 4 he was walking along the quayside by the River Wear when he overbalanced and fell into the water below. Luckily, he was saved from certain drowning by a man named William Wardell, who, heedless of his own safety, dived in to rescue the young boy. Thirteen years later, Douglas was working with his father on the keelboats, when one day a ship named *Ajax* was wrecked off Sunderland. Douglas alone made three trips in his keel to the stricken ship, rescuing all of the crew. Amongst those that he rescued was William Wardell.

But perhaps the most miraculous of our short list of maritime preservations occurred during the great flood of 1771, when the northern rivers were swollen to levels never before seen. The old Tyne Bridge was washed away. In Durham City, Elvet Bridge collapsed into the raging torrent that was the River Wear and at South Shields a vessel lying just offshore rescued a baby, alive and well, which was floating out to sea still in its wooden cradle.

n

This tale is set in an age which now, like a common collective memory, seems at once somehow familiar and yet still strangely distant. It is set at a time which, though coal mining had begun, certainly pre-dates the introduction of the intensive mining and ironworks which would later come to scar the countryside around Tudhoe and Spennymoor. Indeed, the story has resonances of a more remote, bygone age of rural life, of 'Olde England' and of rustic ceremonies, the symbolism of which had its roots in an even more ancient, pagan past.

The scene of the drama, Nicky Nack Wood, no longer exists. Only two remnants of that original forest have survived the ravages of industrialisation. One small wood, Tudhoe Wood, lies to the south of the inn at Croxdale (now known as the Daleside Arms, for generations this inn was known as the Nicky Nack). The other, Croxdale Wood, stretches away in the opposite direction almost as far as the River Wear.

So our story begins in a time, as the *Monthly Chronicle* tells us 'when the township was entirely rural, and the principal inhabitants, besides the vicar, were the farmers who occupied the eight local farms'.

The day had been long; the last day of reaping. The workers in the fields had been in good spirits, entertained by musicians whom the farmer had paid to come and play. As the warm day wore on, some had even broken out into dance, fuelled no doubt by the anticipation of the drinking and feasting to come later. But now, temporarily exhausted by their exertions, they waited; waited for the last cut of the day, on the last farm, at the end of the harvest. This day was the one honoured above all others and marked the feast of Harvest Home, also known as Mell Day. Above all they awaited the traditional merriment which would take place later that night: the Mell Supper.

Sheaves of corn had been bound and placed, as tradition dictated, in stooks of twelve, the golden bounty glowing in the late summer sun. All now gathered for the traditional climax to the day; they gathered in the last field, the Nicky Nack Field, anticipating the very final cut of the harvest. Laughter and song filled the air; the merrymaking was about to begin. The reapers turned their backs on the wood that stood hard by the field, for the Nicky Nack Wood was a dark place which nobody much cared for. It seemed to those honest workers on that happy, glowing, glorious evening, that the wood silently watched them, with root and branch reaching out into the field, seemingly in envy, as if trying to grasp and extinguish the sunlight and merriment there.

The final cut was made and in time-honoured fashion, the farmer gave the traditional instruction: 'Shout the Mell.' The reapers, as their forefathers had done since times long distant, threw their hooks into the air, joined hands to form the welkin ring and chanted the response: 'Blest be the day that Christ was born, we've getten't mell of farmer's corn, weel bound and better shorn.' The ancient verse echoed across the field but fell stifled under the trees. The last sheaf of corn cut was gathered up by a young maid and plaited into the likeness of a child's doll. Then, ornamented with colourful ribbons, the kern babby was ceremonially carried off towards the lowering sun, and on to the place of the Mell Supper; leaving the wood to the shadows and the night.

This night's feast would be the last of the eight. Harvest was already home at the other nearby farms. The same workers had seen it completed at Tudhoe Hall and Tudhoe North Farm. They had shouted the Mell over the fields at High Butcher Race and at Coldstream and enjoyed Mell Suppers at them all, especially the previous one at Tudhoe Moor. But this Mell Supper at Tudhoe Mill, the last of the season, promised to be special. Many looked forward to the long night ahead. None could have foreseen just how long the night would be.

The supper was indeed going well. Plentiful supplies of food and a seemingly endless flow of ale and spirits had made for a high time. Talk was loud and mainly of the harvest and many a glass was raised. As the night drew on, the singing became louder, the rhymes coarser, the dancing more frenzied and, upon it all, the kern babby gazed down from her lofty place of honour. As the drink and the day's exertions began to take their toll, groups of workers began to settle, and the subject and tone of their drunken conversations began to darken. At length, the talk turned to Nicky Nack Wood. Many admitted that they had felt ill at ease as the last cut of corn had been made, and as tongues were loosened by drink, stories began to be told, revealing half-remembered legends of the wood and its reputation.

One reveller related that the wood had got its name after a traveller, who, whilst passing through it, had thought he heard a clicking sound echoing behind him. Someone or something was trying to catch him! He ran, but the faster he ran, the faster the nameless, invisible thing, for so it was, followed. 'Nicky nack, nicky nack' was the sound it made, or so said the traveller, and it was not until he'd passed through the wood, and emerged safely from the other side, that he'd realised the sound of a loose heel plate on his own boot was the explanation for the invisible phantom from which he'd fled in terror.

It was a story that never failed to raise a guffaw of ridicule. That said, however, the local people knew that the wood did have a reputation. Those living in the countryside thereabouts thought it a bad and disturbed wood. They did not know why, but they sensed that there was something not quite right with it. Secretive it seemed, as if watching, waiting. Most simply chose not to go there, if it could be avoided, and then never at night. They felt uneasy, both with it, and in it. Others, however, went further, for they were entirely convinced that some dark, ghostly thing walked under the ancient twisted trees of the Nicky Nack Wood.

A loud oath, heavy with the influence of ale, rang out across the farm kitchen. The unthinkable had happened. The drink had run out. Neither a drop of ale, nor a drop of brandy was left to sustain the reapers for the hours still to come.

Curses and accusations rang in the air. Whose fault had it been? It was the farmer's fault; too damned mean with his brandy! It was the reapers' fault; drinking more than was good for them! Some left in disgust, growling under their breath that this Mell Supper had been the worst of them all; they would think twice about coming back to this farm next year. Then above the bellowed recriminations that flew around the room, a suggestion was made, which was quickly agreed to by everyone who remained. They would send someone out to get more supplies. There would be some to get at Sunderland Bridge and it wouldn't take that long to get there and back.

A young farmhand, who had previously been sitting getting quietly drunk, as he'd listened, transfixed, to the dark stories of Nicky Nack Wood, now realised that he'd been volunteered to go and get supplies of brandy from Sunderland Bridge. However, to get there, he must first pass through that same dread wood. Nonetheless, the young lad, fired up no doubt with liquid courage, dutifully set about his task and made off for Sunderland Bridge. Before him, brooding in the distance, still and quiet, lay the dense mass of the wood, standing black and frowning in the moonlight.

But ale and brandy had fortified him against any nightly fears. Across the moonlit fields he tramped, breathing in great gulps of the cool, pungent night air. He looked upward, if a little unsteadily, and gawped at the ink-black sky, bejewelled with myriad shimmering stars. His spirits were high and they were not much lowered as he crossed under the outermost overhanging boughs of the wood. Once inside, the moonlight, bright and emboldening on the outside, became dimmed. It seemed that the grudging trees would allow no more than the most feeble and translucent fingers of light to touch the forest floor.

Still, nothing deterred the intrepid messenger. He looked around, his eyes quickly growing accustomed to the darkness. He breathed in the air of the wood. But the air was different here and seemed damp and earthy. Scents wafted into his nostrils and gave hints of the mould and decay of an autumn which would soon cover all. He listened. The quiet calm of the wood was broken only by the sound of his boots thudding in the darkness and the noises of woodland creatures going about their nightly business. Shrieks and yelps came from the dimness and may have unnerved a night-time traveller less experienced in country ways than he. However, his was a soul close to nature and he recognised the owl and the fox and, knowing that the noises he heard had natural origins, no imaginings of his would turn them into wild fancies of nameless horrors stalking the wood. He began to feel at ease, to slow his pace, to dawdle, trying to pick out and identify, with his ale-dulled senses, every sound of the woodland night. Time slipped by.

At Tudhoe Mill, tempers were beginning to fray. Where was the boy? He should have been back by now! The earlier good humour of the night had turned ugly. One man, who earlier had been sharing the stories of Nicky Nack Wood with which the young farmhand had been so enthralled, 'swore a dark oath that he would go and fetch the boy back, by the lug', and at the same time, give him such a fright that he would never again waste time on so vital an errand. To this effect he procured a white linen sheet, so that he could assume the very image of the dreaded Nicky Nack Ghost. Then he set off for the wood, there to lay in wait for the unsuspecting young errand boy.

The lad had been held in conversation at Sunderland Bridge, his tales of the Mell Day, the evening's merriment and the farmer running out of drink causing much amusement. More time slipped by, until at length, with his empty vessels suitably – even generously – replenished and with much waving of hands and many offers of thanks, he started out on his return journey to Tudhoe Mill. Soon he plunged back into Nicky Nack Wood. The familiar noises started again, almost as a welcome back, or so it seemed to him. The same shrieks and yelps he'd identified before returned to greet him and when the sound of water came to his ears, he smiled to himself. He stepped lightly on the stones that served as a crossing over the beck that trickled steadily through the wood and he remembered the old lore which told that if any evil thing followed, it could not pass over running water. He heeded not what might lay in wait on the other side.

Instead the music, light and merriment of the night's earlier proceedings now filled his thoughts. He recalled the blank but approving gaze of the kern babby watching the revelries and the reapers regaled with good ale. The strong ale, made all the more potent by the addition of a liberal supply from the brandy bottle, had been enjoyed by all and the heady mixture had sent home early, chirping merrily, some of the young maids and ancient dames of the village. Another treat had been the dancers, the mummers and guisers in their fantastical costumes; he didn't know what it was all supposed to mean, but he'd enjoyed it mightily.

All at once he froze, as if pierced by an icy knife. With a sudden, dreadful realisation, he was aware of what his ears had been hearing but what his brain had been oblivious to. The familiar animal noises of the wood had ceased and had been silent for some time. Then, with a sudden surge of terror, he was aware that something was approaching him, flitting unnaturally between the thin shafts of moonlight that struggled down through the trees. Some shrouded white thing that at first seemed to be on the road ahead of him. No! Now it was alongside, watching him, moving with him. A dread, half-seen figure with what seemed through the darkness to be two arms outstretched towards him. The ghoulish apparition appeared to be toying with him, mocking him, before inevitably bearing down on the horrified boy. The stories of Nicky Nack Wood, he now realised to his dismay, were true. He ran forward, blindly at first, not daring to look over his shoulder for fear of the advancing horror. But look he soon did, and he saw a very curious thing.

When neither the boy nor his would-be tormentor returned to Tudhoe Mill, some, even amongst the most hardened revellers, resigned themselves to the fact that the night was finally over and began to trudge their weary way home.

Others, a little nervously, wondered what could have befallen their two wayfarers of the night. They would soon be enlightened as the bedraggled figure of the exhausted and terrified boy clattered through the farmhouse door. He was of course questioned at once about what had happened, but those privy to the prank did not yet want to give the game away. With the wink of an eye and with knowing smiles on their lips, they asked the unfortunate lad if he'd 'seen anything', for to be sure he looked as if he'd seen a ghost! 'Aye, that aa have', was the reply and he began to tell his tale.

He told how, as he had been coming through the wood, quite close by the Nicky Nack Field, a spectre all of white had appeared and had come at him, 'and aa was sair freeten'd'. The men smiled at the obvious success of their friend's trick and wondered where he could be. But their smiles swiftly faded as the boy continued. He revealed that, as he had turned to look, a second phantom had appeared and 'Aa saw a black ghost ahint it'. Then, in his terror, and for no reason known to him, he called out to the black ghost to catch the white one: 'And the white ghost leukt about, and when it saw the black yen, it screamed out amain.' And its screams, he went on, were terrible: 'But blackey was ower clivvor for it and went like a hatter, till it gat haud o' whitey, and went away with 'im aaltogivvor.'

The faces of the gathered company were pale now. Their friend had still not returned and in the unfolding of the tale, the night sky had begun to lighten and the mists of morning now enshrouded the scene of the drama. They resolved to wait for full daylight before attempting to establish the fate of the young farmhand's tormentor. Sometime later, close to the eaves of the wood and covered by a few early fallen leaves, they found a few torn fragments of white linen: 'But what became of the man himself, could never be ascertained.'

Some have explained the story thus. That the tormentor, mindful himself of the stories of the wood, on hearing the farmhand's cry for help, looked around and saw his own shadow cast by the shafts of moonlight. Instantly believing it to be some vengeful apparition, he ran away, screaming in terror. The boy simply witnessed the optical illusion of the man's shadow 'catching up with him' and carrying him away. It was suspected that, in his blind flight, he had perhaps fallen down some old shaft to be forever lost.

The story itself may be apocryphal and shares a common motif with other such ghost tales including a very similar story from Netherbury, in Dorset. Perhaps such tales were intended to serve as a warning to the curious or the frivolous, advising them to show proper respect to the supernatural. Whatever the meaning or origin of this story, it is a known fact that the celebration of Mell Day went on in the region well into the nineteenth century. The antiquarian Michael Aislabie Denham recorded that in the 1820s he saw reapers returning from the Mell Field in the evening 'dressed in high crowned muslin caps, profusely ornamented with ribbons of various colours, and preceded by music'. The tale of Nicky Nack Wood comes, therefore, from a bygone age of rural living when the area was rife with superstitious beliefs. Certainly this was a time when Tudhoe Village alone was believed to be the haunt of a number of well-documented (if dubious) apparitions, mostly of the animal kind. Stories such as these would gradually be forgotten and lost to successive, more industrialised and enlightened generations, until finally the nineteenth-century chroniclers declared that: 'With the spread of education, and the great influx of strangers into the district to carry on the coal mining and iron industries, they have now mostly faded out of recollection, and are beyond hope of recovery.'

Well perhaps!

The author, living as a child of the twentieth century in that part of the county, and going to school close to the scene of the story, was always aware of the ghostly tales told of Nicky Nack Wood. The little school we attended as inquisitive 9 and 10 year olds was situated quite close by Tudhoe Wood, a surviving remnant of its legendary predecessor. As children we would think nothing of roaming the nearby fields and hedgerows in boyish pursuits. But we never passed beyond the eaves of Tudhoe Wood. It always had a reputation. Nobody much cared for it. Secretive it seemed, as if watching, waiting. Some said it was haunted. Of course we didn't really believe that; we simply chose not to go there!

❧ NUTS TO THE VICAR ❧

On the evening of Sunday, 16 March 1851, the vicar of St Oswald's church in Durham City retired to his vestry to count the Evensong collection money and was surprised by a curious but nonetheless welcome alternative to his congregation's usual offerings.

On first examination of the collection plate it was immediately apparent that there, in the midst of the familiar coinage, was a walnut; just an ordinary walnut,

St. Oswald's Church, Durham.

of normal shape and size and apparently whole and sound. Perhaps an offering in kind from someone who had no coin to give or, more likely, simply a gift from a parishioner: a rather strange but 'unconsidered trifle'.

But, waste not, want not! And the vicar, presumably being rather partial to walnuts, split open the shell in order to consume the offering. However, his curiosity was immediately aroused on finding inside the broken shell, not the kernel, but what seemed to be a small parcel of white paper. He began to unwrap it. He found that a first layer of paper enclosed another, which enclosed another, which enclosed another and that inside of all were set two more pieces of paper, compressed into the smallest possible dimensions. Gently unfolding them, he discovered to his astonishment that they were in fact two £5 notes and, on a slip of paper wrapped with them, there were the words: 'A nut for the Vicar to crack!'

In 1851, a donation of £10 to the church collection was no doubt a significant contribution indeed, and as Fordyce put it in his recording of the incident: 'What a happy mortal it must be, who can afford to crack such racy jokes as these.'

⚜ OLD SUNDERLAND BRIDGE ⚜

Old Sunderland Bridge is a pretty spot, especially on a quiet, misty, spring morning or a warm summer's afternoon.

There has been a crossing over the River Wear here since medieval times and probably since even before that. The bridge which now spans the water, Old Sunderland Bridge, 3 miles south of Durham City, was once described as 'perhaps the narrowest bridge on the whole of the Great North Road'. Armies at war, mail coaches, highwaymen, seekers after adventure or knowledge and solitary travellers simply going about their business, have all passed by this way travelling countless footsteps along that once great highway.

Today, the Great North Road, the modern A167, is carried over the River Wear by a new road bridge which was constructed in 1925. The Old Bridge, a little way upstream, now sees little activity, though visitors may drive their cars across it to park up and set off idly on one of the several picturesque walks nearby. Anglers wander through the scene to pursue their solitary and contemplative craft. Visitors to nearby Croxdale Hall, home of the Salvin family, and occasional estate and farm vehicles make up the remaining traffic. A short way upstream, the rude, red-brick Victorian viaduct has, since 1872, carried the East Coast main railway line high over the river valley.

In spring and autumn, sightseers come to look over the low parapets of the Old Bridge and watch the annual runs of salmon and sea trout returning from the sea to their spawning grounds high up in Weardale. Many spend time there in quiet contemplation, staring long into the rushing foam, entranced by the siren call of the water as it glides between the venerable cutwaters and rumbles and rolls out over the weirs below.

There are few visitors to the scene at night.

In the summer of 1327, an English army under the command of the 14-year-old King Edward III, marching south from Durham City, crossed the River Wear at this spot in pursuit of an invading Scottish army under the Earl of Douglas. And it was here again, on an October day almost twenty years later, that the bloodied and rent survivors of the Scottish skirmishing party escaped across the river in the other direction. Behind them they left the remains of 500 of their countrymen, slaughtered by the English cavalry on what came to be known as Butcher Race about 2 miles to the south. Those survivors who made it across the bridge would meet their final, fatal destiny and the annihilation of their army at the Battle of Neville's Cross.

Old Sunderland Bridge, near Croxdale.

In 1602, the highwayman, Andrew Tate, was hung at the top of the hill a short distance to the south, 'where the Darlington and Auckland roads diverge'. Afterwards he was 'buried beneath the gallows', his punishment for robbing and murdering several people at nearby Burn Hall. Little surprise then that, over the centuries, stories have emerged from travellers along the road at Old Sunderland Bridge of strange and sometimes alarming nocturnal experiences. At night it certainly seems an admirable and appropriate place for a haunting and local tradition suggests that this is indeed so, with a number of half-remembered tales of something looming in the dark. Sometimes the figure of a man has been whispered about; a solitary watcher, distinct, motionless, staring from the parapet down into the rushing blackness below. Sometimes it is nothing more substantial than a shadow, some deeper darkness on an otherwise dark night. At other times, travellers crossing the bridge at night have experienced a vague but nonetheless unnerving feeling of not being entirely alone in their apparent isolation.

Eerie and unsettling it has always been, but those who have been witness to it have never reported the feeling of shock or panic more commonly associated with such meetings in the night. Melancholy, not terror, seems to pervade the nocturnal atmosphere around Old Sunderland Bridge and envelop night-time travellers, like the mist rising from the cold water below.

At the end of the eighteenth century, the occupier of Tudhoe Mill was returning home late after a visit to Durham City. Crossing the Old Bridge, he looked up Croxdale Bank ahead of him, and saw 'A stiff built, tallish man, trudging up the road'. It seemed that the stranger was wearing a broad-brimmed hat of the type favoured by Quakers and perhaps he was indeed a Quaker, or perhaps he was something else entirely. Because of the location, the miller felt that he would be glad of some company and increased his pace. But try as he might, he couldn't catch up with the mysterious wayfarer. He followed the phantom figure up the bank, always with the same distance between them, passed the site of Andrew Tate's execution and walked as far along the Auckland Road as Nicky Nack Bridge. Here the mysterious figure simply vanished. For the rest of his days the miller would always insist that the figure he had encountered that night crossing the Old Bridge had been a ghost, an insistence for which he was roundly ridiculed.

The morning of 16 June 1821 dawned pleasant and sunny. The mail coach to London was full, both of mail and of paying passengers. It was a fine day so Mr Chater, a solicitor from Newcastle, and Mr Samuel Whitaker, from Bingley in Yorkshire, were happy to ride on the roof alongside the driver and the guard. They were joined before the mail coach left by Mr Thomas Donaldson, a native of Perthshire, and a number of other passengers who decided to travel inside.

The driver, James Auld, was no doubt aware that, with fine weather and firm conditions under horses and wheels, good time could be made. The London mail coach set off from Durham City and thundered south down the Great North Road.

Over the bridge towards Croxdale Bank.   'A sharp left turn.'

Shortly afterwards it crossed the small bridge over the River Browney, where, in 1694, the racing Squire Sockeld had crashed his steed through the bridge wall and fallen into the water below, giving rise to the rather obscure local anecdote of 'Sockeld's Leap'. Miraculously, injury was sustained by neither horse nor rider. Over Browney Bridge they went and Auld sped his team towards the River Wear and the Old Bridge, a mere bow-shot away.

A sharp right turn was required and then a sharp left onto the bridge itself: 'The turn at the north end is very abrupt, and the parapet is by no means superfluously high'. But Auld was driving too fast. As he approached the left turn onto the bridge he became aware – too late – of a horse and rider turning onto the bridge at the same time on his inside. In order to avoid them he tried to swing wide to the right, and then back to the left, to regain the road over the bridge. But Auld misjudged the tight turn and lost control. It was a misjudgement that would have tragic consequences.

The coach overturned and smashed into the bridge parapet. Auld himself and the guard were thrown between the horses and the parapet wall. Mr Chater, also on the top of the coach, managed somehow to cling on and thus survived. However, Mr Whitaker and Mr Donaldson were not so fortunate. They were thrown over the bridge parapet on the upstream side, falling the 30ft or so to the river below and were dashed off the bridge cutwaters. Donaldson was killed on the spot.

Whitaker survived for four hours before he also died. The remaining passengers who had also begun their journey that day, inside the coach, received no injury. The deceased were interred in Brancepeth churchyard on 23 June and the service, we are told, was attended by 'a large concourse of people'. James Auld was found guilty of manslaughter at the August Assizes in Durham City and he was sentenced to nine months in prison, but was released in February 1822.

Who knows? Perhaps the sad victims of that day's tragedy occasionally return to the scene of their demise. But surely, the Sunderland Bridge coach crash occurred in the bright summer time, when, on happier days, many would visit 'the lovely woodland borders of the Wear at this spot, where it is safe to linger and drink in the beauty of the scene, and where the exceedingly picturesque old stone bridge of four arches carries the road over the river'.

The scene of the tragedy.

Still, it seems to be a place to be avoided in the night time and generations have given the Old Bridge a wide berth during the hours of darkness.

❖ ONLAFBAL THE PAGAN ❖

There is a story from medieval times about a thief who hid in Durham Cathedral in order to steal treasures from the shrine of St Cuthbert. The first part of his plan went well and before the day darkened, he had successfully concealed himself from the guardian monks. Next morning, however, he was discovered, lying flat, as if pinned to the floor, alive but unable to move. Unable to even speak, his guilt was proved when the treasures he had intended to take were discovered on his person. The great saint, it seemed, was unforgiving of those who would wrong him.

A better-known story tells of how the mighty William the Conqueror himself fled from Durham in terror, leaving untouched a great banquet that had been prepared for him. He had questioned the truth of accounts of the incorruptible body of the saint. He did not believe them and had demanded to see the incorrupt body with his own eyes, promising that he would execute all those who presumed to

Bow Lane, Durham City, the site of the King's Gate.   The scene of William the Conqueror's flight?

deceive him. On approaching St Cuthbert's shrine, however, he was suddenly seized with a violent fever – clearly a demonstration of the saint's displeasure. The dread king fled in fear, mounted his horse and sped from Durham, never reining back his horse until he had reached the River Tees. Even the mightiest, it seemed, ignored at their peril the wrath of St Cuthbert.

The early tenth century was a troubled time in the North and East of England. Viking raiders seemed to be here to stay and conquering warlords divided out the spoils, the riches and the land. After his victory at the Battle of Corbridge in AD 918, the Danish Viking chieftain, Ragnald, divided the land that he now occupied between two of his loyal war captains: Scula and Onlafbal. But the land in question lay between the rivers Tyne and Tees, representing most of what is now County Durham, and was considered to be the sacred Patrimony of St Cuthbert, the land of St Cuthbert himself.

And so, the monkish chronicler Simeon of Durham tells us, Onlafbal, or possibly Onlaf the Bold, 'proceeded to such a height of insolence as to seize land of the Bishopric. He treated the Bishop, who wished to save a sinner more than to recover his possessions, with the utmost contempt, and uttered the most profane blasphemies against St Cuthbert.' This, no doubt, sealed his fate!

Being angered by the stories of the power of St Cuthbert, Onlafbal set out to prove who was the mightier: 'why do you threaten me with your dead man?

I swear by the power of my Gods, I will be a fearful enemy both to this dead man and to all of you.' He soon made his way to Chester-le-Street, where St Cuthbert's body then lay, intending to throw down the saint's shrine and take what he could, proving to all that he was indeed the mightier. But as he entered through the doorway, he suddenly stood rigid, as if nailed by both feet to the threshold. Signs of agony began to show on his face and very soon he seemed to be suffering 'extreme torture'. Unable to move, he collapsed to the floor where, uttering his final words and, according to Simeon, acknowledging 'the power and sanctity of St Cuthbert', he expired without further ado.

His warrior band quickly fled and would soon tell their compatriots of how the mighty Onlafbal had met his fate. When word of the events reached Scula, he decided that in the face of such powerful magic, discretion was the better option. He and his men boarded their ships and returned 'whence they came'.

The actual historical events surrounding Onlafbal's death were no doubt embellished by Simeon, writing at a later date at Durham, to emphasise the power of St Cuthbert and the power of the blessed over the aggression of the heathen. This would also have served to reinforce the growing cult of St Cuthbert, attracting more pilgrims with their offerings to his holy shrine.

Of course, the modern reader could doubtless think of a number of medical reasons which may have brought about Onlafbal's death and the symptoms could be said to describe a heart attack, a stroke or perhaps a brain haemorrhage. But as far as Simeon of Durham was concerned, there was only one explanation for the seemingly inexplicable demise of Onlaf the Bold: the mighty Viking chieftain had been seen off by the dead man and the heathen marauders 'left the possessions of the church free for evermore'.

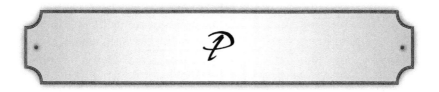

⚜ PRIVATEERS ⚜

We probably all have an image of how pirates should look and sound. This might be, as perhaps for older readers, the fictional Long John Silver of Robert Louis Stevenson's *Treasure Island* as imagined and carefully constructed by the actor Robert Newton, or the modern-day vision of pirates as portrayed in the Hollywood franchise *Pirates of the Caribbean*. We may also have heard stories about real-life pirates with the names of Edward Teach, known to history as Blackbeard, and the notorious captains Morgan and Kidd.

However, from the sixteenth to the eighteenth century, privateers were also active upon the world's oceans. Essentially legalised pirates, they sailed, or owned, armed ships and held a license, known as Letters of Marque, from the monarch or government. This license gave them permission to attack with impunity, to steal from or take as a prize, ships of the Spanish fleet or the French fleet, or whoever happened to be the enemy of the day. So it was that ordinary shipowners could secure legal approval, enabling them to arm their own vessels and seek their own fortune upon the high seas, essentially by stealing someone else's.

Though it has a coastline and is therefore officially considered a maritime county, it probably has to be said that readers might not automatically associate County Durham with pirates. However, prominent among the privateers were the shipowners of Sunderland who, we are told, lost no time at all in arming their vessels, which they then sailed in predatory groups, affording them both advantage and mutual protection.

But curiously, it wasn't just a male enterprise. There were of course female pirates, with the likes of Anne Bonny and Mary Read being just as ruthless as their male counterparts. Furthermore, there is record of a company being formed to undertake a serious privateering enterprise which was entirely made up of ladies, who sought out, and were granted the support of the Countess of Northumberland who acted as their patron. An early effort, perhaps, to promote women's equality. The object of these good ladies was recorded in the company prospectus and directed them to 'purchase, man, fit out and employ, three private ships of war'. The capital investment was '200 shares of £100 each'.

In return, the prospectus went on to say that half the net produce of all prizes taken 'is to be equally divided among the subscribers, the other half to be distributed between the crews of the ships according to their respective shares'. None, moreover, 'were to be permitted to subscribe' to the enterprise 'but a lady's name'.

The privateering system, piracy underwritten by legality, was perhaps unsurprisingly 'marvellously popular' as massive profits, even fortunes, could be made. And in County Durham, many of the cannons manufactured for these enterprises were made at the Whitehall works, near Chester-le-Street.

In the end though, the golden age of the privateers, like that of the pirates, came and went. But at least some of the guns made at Chester-le-Street were salvaged and turned to more peaceful purposes. Set upright (muzzle end downward), they were, we are told, sunk at street corners for the protection of the narrow public thoroughfares of Sunderland.

❖ PUNISHMENT AND HUMILIATION ❖

In County Durham, long before the system of justice with which we are familiar today was introduced, the Halmote Court was a means of enforcing the prince bishop's laws and dispensing his justice upon individuals found guilty of lesser crimes and breaches of the peace. Brought before the court would be those accused of the most common of affrays. These included the drawing of knives and wounding in quarrels, public drunkenness and 'incontinence' (unrestrained sexual activity), for which there was a special fine. All such activities would lead to punishments specifically designed for the 'ignominious exposure of offenders and the correction of rogues and malefactors'.

Punishments and public humiliations for a wide variety of crimes would be common across the County Palatine. Today some of them perhaps seem bizarre, perhaps even comic, but they were also cruel and painful, with records describing how 'rogues and vagabonds are often stocked and whipped; scolds are ducked upon the Ducking Stools in the water'.

Indeed, one of the most common sentences passed by the Halmote Court was the ducking of women. Though not exclusively a punishment for females, it was most often used to 'harness the unruly and malicious tongues of scolding dames'. Essentially, a scold was a woman who had any, all, or a combination of the following attributes: loud, aggressive, argumentative, interfering, often accused of ceaselessly complaining and of spreading slanderous gossip about her neighbours. Basically minding everyone else's business, as well as her own! Ducking stools, known variously as cuckstools or tumbrils, were a common sight across the county and it was a civic responsibility of town or village to provide one.

In 1627, the worthies of Gateshead were fined for not having one and the same punishment was meted out at South Shields.

James J. Dodd, in his *History of the Urban District of Spennymoor*, tells of the ducking stool in Tudhoe Village. It stood opposite the Old Hall, at the edge of the (now long filled in) village pond: 'This was a pole fixed in the pond, with a transverse beam upon it, turning on a swivel, with a chair at the end of it. Any woman who caused strife in the village, or intermeddled unlawfully in her neighbour's affairs, was turned around, and the scolding or slanderous dame ducked in the pond.'

The actual apparatus was either permanently fixed near a suitable body of water, quite often the village pond, or was capable of being stored elsewhere and trundled along to the scene of punishment, for 'the scoulds to be duckt over the head and ears'.

As it was part of the Halmote Court's regular business, it was common for a 'Proper Officer' (usually a parish official) to be in attendance to ensure that the sentence of the court was carried out. This official would formally process to the scene of the punishment 'with the parish rabble at his heels', eager no doubt, for spectacle and entertainment. Another essential individual present would be a figure, somewhat less dreaded than the public executioner, known as the public 'Dukar in the Watter' who would actually carry out the sentence and would be paid for his expertise in the use of the apparatus. And so it was that 'men and women alike, who could not bridle their tongues, were in peril of a muddy bath'.

As an old poem relates:

> There stands, my friend, in yonder pool,
> An engine called a Ducking Stool;
> By legal power condemned down,
> The joy and terror of the town;
> If jarring females kindle strife,
> Give language foul or lug the coif;
> If noisy dames should once begin,
> To drive the house with horrid din;
> 'Away! you cry, 'You'll grace the stool,
> We'll teach you how your tongue to rule.'

Of course, a ducking was not always a direct result of the judgement of the court. In 1626 a curate of Chester-le-Street, a seemingly less than sympathetic personage, had an eye to make himself a dwelling from the anchorage attached to the church. Unfortunately, in accordance with custom, it was already occupied and being used as an almshouse by some poor widows of the parish, who refused to vacate it in favour of the clergyman. Undaunted, the curate obtained his own warrant to 'eject them; and give them a ducking'. However, public sensibilities were outraged, the old dames were provided with 'a barr to the inner door' and with the combined opposition of the parish and of 'three strong men', their eviction never took place. But occasionally a community itself would take direct action, regardless of law and 'licensed hands', and some poor woman upon whom their displeasure had fallen would suffer the watery torment, being carried off by the mob and lawlessly dipped, 'regardless of her cries'.

Eventually, however, the ducking stool fell out of fashion and it was replaced as a popular punishment by the branks, or scold's bridle. This horrendous device, 'much preferred to the Ducking Stool', was essentially a simple iron frame which was fitted over the head of the victim. It incorporated a rough iron gag for the mouth and the whole device was attached to something akin to a dog lead. The gag itself was described by a commentator, writing in 1772 (by which time it seems that attitudes were beginning to change), as being 'as sharp as a chisel, which cut the poor female till blood gushed from each side of her mouth.' He questioned 'not only the inhumanity, but the legality of the practice'.

The bizarre and somewhat comical sight of the drunkard's cloak was also witnessed in public. It was simply a barrel into which the torso of a habitual inebriate would be fastened, with his arms outstretched and his hands restrained, protruding at either side.

The ducking stool.

The scold's bridle and the drunkard's cloak.

Of course the stocks and the pillory are, perhaps as a result of various historical TV series or popular movies, still familiar to, if often confused by, today's generations. And indeed, physical examples of both still survive; some original, some modern recreations. In centuries past, most villages and towns would have them as simple devices to punish and publicly humiliate offenders, and they would be a feature of village greens, market places and any other location where a community would come together. The popular image of them, which seems still to be embedded in the public consciousness, is probably that of some unfortunate locked in the stocks or in the pillory and being pelted by the great unwashed with rotten fruit, rotten vegetables or some other, even more noisome material.

The length of time a miscreant would be locked in would depend upon the seriousness of the crime committed. Some spent just a few hours. In 1685 it is recorded that one John Ornsby, found guilty of perjury, stood for an hour in the pillory in Durham Market Place. Other sentences were more prolonged (perhaps lasting for days on end), with the victim, as well as being exposed to the attentions of the mob, suffering prolonged physical pain, the effects of thirst and hunger and perhaps even a whipping.

Perhaps the cruellest and most sinister implement of punishment, used both in public and behind closed doors, was the whipping post. Variations of the device were known as the whipping stool or whipping ladder, but though its physical nature sometimes varied, its grim function always remained the same. The following is an account of a punishment meted out in Durham Prison as late as the second half of the nineteenth century:

The Whipping ladder consisted of two uprights, joined by a crossbar of iron, with a moveable pad to support the chest of the man being flogged. The Governor, the Surgeon, the Chief Warder and two others are at hand. One of the two Warders who are to share the duty of flogging holds a 'Cat', a handle of some eighteen inches long with nine thongs of knotted whipcord about a yard and a half long. The first prisoner is brought out. John Henry Pryor, a twenty five year old Boilersmith, is one of the half dozen highway robbers sentenced at the Assizes three weeks ago. He and James Carabine, a twenty five year old labourer, were each condemned to fifteen years penal servitude and twenty five strokes of the lash, for highway robbery at Stockton.

Four young pitmen were also sentenced, for systematically robbing travellers along a lonely road between Durham and Neville's Cross.

This was on Friday, 13 March, 1874.

Of course, all these methods of trial and torment were eventually, mercifully, consigned to history. The *Monthly Chronicle* of 1888 reflects that 'Ducking Stools and Branks, however, with all their terrors, seem to have been insufficient to frighten the shrews of former days out of their bad propensities. Society has come to the conclusion that there is no cure for the fiery tongue in cold water, or cold iron either, and has laid them both aside'.

But James J. Dodd, writing only nine years later and perhaps with his mind wandering back to the long gone ducking stool in Tudhoe Village, dared to suggest, probably mischievously, that 'there are people in Spennymoor today, who would gladly see this admirable institution revived'.

The pillory around 1812.   The stocks and the whipping post.

⁓ PYRAMID ⁓

In the 1953 edition of the rather fulsomely titled *The King's England: Durham – A Guide to everything that makes the County famous, Town by Town, Village by Village* we are reminded, if we were not already fully aware, that two of the County Palatine's parish churches have a curious connection with a pharaoh of Ancient Egypt and one of the Seven Wonders of the World.

George Elliot was born in 1815, in Penshaw. His father was a pitman and, at the age of 9, George followed him down Whitefield Colliery, as a trapper boy. As he grew, he used part of his wages to pay for a night school education, studying surveying and mine engineering. It paid off and George soon began to rise through the ranks, eventually becoming one of the chief agents of Lord Londonderry. He bought financial interests in a number of collieries, eventually purchasing his own outright, and, in 1864, he became the proud new owner of Whitefield Colliery, where he had begun his working life as a trapper boy forty years before.

Entering politics and becoming Tory MP for North Durham, he was made a baronet in 1874, saw government service and had an interest in Egyptian affairs. He was close to Benjamin Disraeli, advising the prime minister to buy shares in the Suez Canal, therefore giving Great Britain control of the sea route to India. Elliot became financial advisor to the Khedive of Egypt, Ismail Pasha. Eventually, as a permanent reminder of his service, he sought and obtained permission from the Khedive to remove and return to England a block of granite from the Great Pyramid of Giza near Cairo, ancient tomb of the Pharaoh Cheops or Khufu. Elliot had this great block cut into two inscription stones, which served as memorials for the deceased members of his family. One stone went to the church of St Mary, at West Rainton, the other, to All Saints church, Penshaw.

And so it was that nineteenth-century County Durham stonemasons relaid the ancient granite, from the oldest of the Seven Wonders of the Ancient World and the largest pyramid ever built, in the quiet confines of two of County Durham's parish churches. The same granite that had first been laid down in antiquity, by Egyptian artisans, around 4,500 years before.

⚜ QUEER-UNS ⚜

After being held in a lengthy conversation by some eccentric character with unusual, enthusiastically shared and generally unsolicited opinions, the author's late father would say, reflectively, 'by he's a queer-un!'

The following short collection of anecdotes refer to some 'queer-uns' from County Durham's past. The collection is by no means exhaustive but it is, perhaps, representative. The individuals mentioned have little in common save their respective eccentricities and the workhouse which, pointedly, played a part in all their lives.

James Brown had lived, since his youth, in Newcastle and had made an honest living from the cloth trade. He had also written verse, had styled himself the Poet Laureate of Newcastle and would continue to sign himself thus for the rest of his life.

He was always prone to eccentricity but after his first wife, to whom he was devoted, died early, his eccentricities became more marked. In the latter half of the eighteenth century he remarried and moved to Durham City. His new bride was Miss Sarah Richardson, the owner of a theatre and other valuable property in the city and herself 'not devoid of eccentricities'.

Now Brown had both the time and the means to devote himself to writing rather 'dubious' verse, usually of a religious and decidedly apocalyptic nature; verse which we are told had 'neither rhyme nor reason'. Well known around the narrow streets of Durham, Brown 'was in the habit of reciting his effusions', usually to a less than enthusiastic public audience. He was also 'uncommonly susceptible to flattery' and one day, towards the end of his life, he received a large parchment signed, so it seemed, with the GR cipher of the monarch then reigning, George III, and sealed with a large official-looking wax seal. The parchment, a Patent of Nobility, bestowed upon Brown the title Baron Brown of Durham in the County Palatine of Durham; an honour, which he considered, was well overdue. Of course it wasn't genuine, being probably an invention of one or more of the local wags. But it is said that until his dying day 'he never detected the imposture'.

His religious beliefs were unconventional and tended to be blown back and forth, like corn in the wind, meaning that 'he believed in every mad fanatic, who broached opinions contrary to reason and sense'. He also seriously believed that he would not die and would consequently refuse all medical assistance when ill. He declared that, when his time came, he would ascend into heaven physically and visibly; a sight probably never before seen in Durham Market Place and no doubt awaited with great interest. This connection with the divine was further attested by the Archangel Gabriel who, as he told anyone that would listen, had both seen and approved of his work. A curious assertion perhaps, but one which had more to it than one would suspect!

Somewhat bizarrely, there was at the time living in Durham City a young West Indian, who it seems took it upon himself to enter, literally, into Brown's ecstatic, apocalyptic, mystic, personal religious world. He would dress in a white sheet, with goose feathers attached to the shoulders, and visit Brown during the night, purporting to be the Archangel Gabriel. With him he bore letters for Brown, apparently written in heaven by the famed and self-styled religious prophetess Joanna Southcott, who had died in 1814. What's more, he would take back to her Brown's replies. The West Indian eventually left Durham and the credulous Brown was frequently told of the deception. But he would have none of it. Indeed, he once said: 'Did I not see him clearly fly out at the ceiling?'

Brown had his verse published in pamphlet form by publishers at Newcastle and they were offered for sale. Needless to say, he did not make a lot of money. Yet when it was suggested to him that he might do better if he enhanced their outward appearance by having them reproduced in more polished, leather-bound form, like, for example, the volumes of Sir Walter Scott, he declined, insisting that: 'None but the Devil's poets needed fine clothes.'

Eventually, he completed what he considered his finest work: 'his monument more durable than bronze.' It was a pamphlet, published in 1820, with the catchy title: *Poems on Military Battles, Naval Victories, and other important subjects, the most extraordinary ever penned, a Thunderbolt shot from Zion's bow at Satan's Kingdom, the Kingdom of the Devil and the Kingdom of this World reserving themselves in darkness for the great and terrible day of the Lord, as Jude, the servant of the Lord declareth* by James Brown, PL.

It did not sell well!

At the age of 90, he and his wife lost their property and their home and were thrown out into the world 'without a farthing'. Resident for a few months at the Durham Poor House, Brown eventually moved out to live in 'an obscure Inn' where he died, on 11 July 1823, aged 92 and in a state of 'misery and penury'. The nineteenth-century chronicler M.A. Richardson wrote affectionately about Baron Brown of Durham 'who', he said, 'with all his eccentricities, was an honest, harmless and inoffensive old man'.

Billy the Diker was certainly not a poet. Billy, as everyone called him (though nobody knew his real name), lived and worked on the various farms around Washington Village at the end of the nineteenth century. Everyone knew him and he was instantly recognisable, being, we are told, short, fat and unshaven with long unkempt hair. His clothes always appeared too big for him and he always wore leggings made, curiously enough, of straw ropes.

But Billy was highly valued by the local farmers. He would work only for a week at each farm and then move on to the next one. During that week, however, he could turn his hand to any kind of work from ditch digging – which may well explain his rustic soubriquet – to ploughing and from hedge cutting to thatching. All he asked from the farmer was his food, some shelter in a barn or a stable and his pay, in cash, on the Friday. The arrangement worked well and seemed to suit everyone.

After he'd been paid on Friday, Billy made his way into Washington Village to spend his cash. And this he did without exception by purchasing apples, oranges, nuts and whatever sweet treats were available. These he then took to the village green where they would be scrambled, producing a kind of Victorian pick-and-mix for the children of the village. With all the children happy and all Billy's money spent, he would return to his resting place at the local farm. Billy would do this without fail on a Friday and without fail the children would look forward to the bounty from Billy's pay.

There is a biblical saying: 'Give, and it will be given to you.' But sadly, so it seems, not in Billy's case. By definition, the work that he did was gruelling and long. Age and increasing weakness eventually caught up with him and at the last, he was simply too frail to carry on working. But Billy's money had all been spent and the idea of savings would have been very strange to him. Worst of all, he had no home of his own. Nobody offered him any assistance nor even repaid some of the Friday kindness that Billy had shown for as long as could be remembered. There was no alternative for him; he was forced to give up the only life he had known and go into the local workhouse. Soon after becoming resident in that awful place, Billy the Diker died.

The Duke of Baubleshire was not so much a Durham City character as a Durham City institution and daily, as the eighteenth century was drawing to a close, His Grace would promenade the streets of St Cuthbert's city and engage in conversation with those whom he knew or those to whom he could introduce himself. But the dukedom of Baubleshire did not in fact exist and the 'duke' (born Thomas French) had assumed this title solely of his own accord.

French had been, so we are told, an industrious working man until, as the *Monthly Chronicle* gently put it, 'the decline of his understanding'. After this he swiftly rose to his lofty position. To add some sort of substance to his claim, he wore a homemade paper star on the breast of his coat, signifying a noble chivalric order known only to him. His hat was surmounted with a cockade, indicating high military rank, and to complete his outfit he sported 'a liberal display of brass curtail rings on his fingers'.

So around the streets of Durham he would stroll, resplendent in this singular attire and engaging all he could in discussions about affairs of the city, or the State, or the monarchy. He would regale his listeners with accounts of his possessions and the fortunes he generated from the extensive Baubleshire estates: 'though at no time master of a shilling.' And he frequently shared with the patient townsfolk the contents of the 'intimate and frequent correspondence' he had with the king then reigning, George III, regarding affairs of state and the progress of the American Colonial War.

But the Duke of Baubleshire also claimed to have been a past victim of fraud, being robbed, he asserted, of large amounts of cash and bank bills. Consequently, when he noticed a fine and valuable horse or carriage draw up in Durham Market Place, he would invariably accost the hapless owner, claim they were actually property stolen from him and accuse the owner of misappropriation. As such he would prove 'exceedingly annoying to the possessors of the property in dispute', though it must have enlivened more than one dull day in Durham:

> Through Durham daily took his walk
> And talk'd, ye gods how he did talk;
> His private riches, how immense!
> His public virtue, how intense!
> Pre-eminent of all the great,
> His mighty wisdom ruled the State.

The self-proclaimed duke died in the Durham Poor House on 16 May 1796, aged 85. However, so familiar a figure was he that his portrait was lithographed and published before his death. And a short, slightly mocking, poetic epitaph was written about him by an unknown Durham writer, from which the above lines are taken.

Thomas French, the Duke of Baubleshire, was just one of many characters who frequented Durham's old streets and whose 'extraordinary conduct was generally tolerated with good humour'.

Our last queer-un perhaps had fewer eccentricities than the three previously mentioned. His name was William Davison but he was known to all as Billy Fine Day and an anonymous nineteenth-century chronicler saw fit to record a short and affectionate piece about Billy in the *Monthly Chronicle*.

Billy Fine Day had originally been a miner and, in 1843, had survived an underground explosion. But in later life, and for thirty-eight years, he was an inmate of Gateshead Workhouse. Everyone knew him and he was a familiar figure, wheeling his barrow around Gateshead, collecting and gratefully receiving any useful items given by the locals: 'Has thoo an a'ad knife to gie Billy?' In his youth he had been an ardent Dissenter and he would often halt his perambulations to preach and sing to groups of curious urchins. Unfortunately, often when he did this, his barrow would be taken. Still undaunted and with unfailing good humour, he would set off in search of it.

The Duke of Baubleshire.

Billy also had a propensity for smoking. He was always on the cadge and, whatever the weather, he would accost those he knew: 'Gie us a bit weed, it's a fine day; have ye any weed?' If, however, anyone asked him for some, he would say: 'Oh aye, it's a fine day. De as aa de; get aal ye can, and luik for mair.' Mr Penrose, the master of the Gateshead Workhouse, was, somewhat unusually for the time and for someone in his position, a caring man and both he and his wife treated Billy well. If Billy ran out of weed, they would replenish his supply and Billy would often tell of this valued kindness: 'Aa knaa the maister will gie us sum; if he disn't the wife will!'

Billy died at the workhouse on 27 January 1891, but so well known were he and his eccentricities that a song was written about him and sung for many years wherever people met. The unknown chronicler, who recorded Billy's idiosyncrasies in the *Monthly Chronicle* of 1891, hoped in his day that the song telling the tale of Billy Fine Day would 'keep alive his memory for at least a little while'.

It may seem curious in itself that the exploits and eccentricities of these characters would be considered worthy of remembrance in the histories of Durham. But they were and perhaps this short piece will keep the memories of all our queer-uns alive, at least for a little while longer.

⚜ RABY'S SPECTRES ⚜

The great historian of Durham, Robert Surtees, tells us in his mammoth *History and Antiquities of the County Palatine of Durham* about a curious ghost story, one of three supernatural anecdotes concerning Raby Castle, near Staindrop.

The Revd F.J. Hodgson, writing in 1890, said of this magnificent fortress that to the passer-by it presented 'a skyline perhaps unmatched in England' and it is thought that there has been a stronghold on the site of today's Raby Castle since the eleventh century and the reign of the Danish Viking king, Cnut. Certainly popular tradition has it that Bulmer's Tower, the oldest part of the castle, stands on the site of Cnut's own royal hall.

Over the years the fortress was crenellated, added to and became for centuries the County Durham stronghold of the all-powerful Neville family. In 1415 it was the birthplace of Cecily Neville, the 'Rose of Raby', who is no doubt familiar to historians and fans of Philippa Gregory novels alike as the wife of Richard, Duke of York, and the mother of two kings of England: Edward IV and Richard III. Said to be of great beauty, pride and piety, Cecily was active in her husband's cause throughout the Wars of the Roses and it is recorded that her life was 'indissolubly linked with the chief actors in the savage battles, ruthless executions and shameless treasons which stamp the struggle between the rival houses of York and Lancaster'. Of course, as an ancient castle, it is to be expected that Raby should be haunted and, apparently, such expectations are well met.

The sad shade of Charles Neville, 6th (and last) Earl of Westmorland, has reputedly been seen, infrequently, ascending the stairs to the great Barons' Hall. It was here that, on 13 November 1569, the fateful decision was made to commence the Rising of the North; an attempt by the northern Roman Catholic nobles and their supporters, faithful to the Old Religion, to overthrow Queen Elizabeth I, then in the eleventh year of her reign, and replace her with Mary, Queen of Scots. The rising failed and, though escaping execution, the last Earl of Westmoreland was forced to flee to Flanders, there to spend a lifetime in exile until his death in 1601. The tale has since been told that, during the hours of darkness, his ghost journeys back across the sea to Raby. Here it is said to wander in sorrow and longing around the ancient seat of the House of Neville until dawn's light decrees that he must fly back to his lonely Flanders grave.

After the rising, Raby Castle was forfeit to the Crown but was later bought by Sir Henry Vane the Elder. Sir Henry was a courtier to King Charles I; nonetheless, he changed his allegiance during the English Civil War and supported the Parliamentarian cause. His son, Sir Henry Vane the Younger, was a fervent republican, one-time Speaker of the House of Commons and, initially, a close associate of Oliver Cromwell. Described as an 'Intellectual Revolutionary', he eventually fell out with Cromwell and opposed the execution of the king. Following

Coat of arms of Charles Neville, 6th Earl of Westmorland.

Cromwell's death and the Restoration of the Monarchy under King Charles II, Vane remained a committed republican but was promised an amnesty by the new monarch, ostensibly in recognition of his opposition to the execution of the new king's late father. However, the king's promise proved false and Vane was arrested and executed as a traitor. The ghost of Sir Henry Vane the Younger is said by some still to haunt the castle, where he sits forlornly on a chair in the library, opposite a writing desk, from where his severed head silently speaks the words of his final address from the block; prematurely silenced when the axe fell.

As well as the spectres of these two men, who in life were actively involved in some of the major events in our national history, there is also the more curious account of the supposed occupant of a phantom black coach, which, we are told, has occasionally been seen driving up to the castle gate, only to vanish into thin air. In it rides the shade of the first Lady Barnard (A'ad Hell Cat), and it was her strange haunting habits that were thought worthy of mention by Surtees himself. It must be remembered of course, that Robert Surtees had a fertile and mischievous imagination. He invented a number of 'genuine' old legends and ballads which he then sent to his friend, Sir Walter Scott, who would later publish them in good faith as being true.

William Fordyce, writing some decades after Surtees and probably taking a reference from him, tells us that Christopher Vane was created the 1st Baron Barnard of Barnard Castle on 8 July 1699. With his wife Elizabeth he had four sons and four daughters; tragically, two of the sons and three of the daughters died in infancy. In 1714, a bitter and intractable family dispute arose between Lord and

Lady Barnard and their son and heir apparent, Gilbert, upon whom Raby Castle was due to be settled as part of his inheritance. Gilbert had married against his parents' wishes and as a punishment Lord Barnard brought in 200 workmen to strip the castle of its 'iron, glass, doors, floorboards and furniture', cut down the timber in the park, kill the deer and strip the lead from the roof 'to a value of £3,000'.

The aggrieved Gilbert was subsequently granted an injunction against his parents, to stop further damage to his inheritance. The injunction also decreed that the castle should be repaired to the same condition in which it had previously been. A commission was appointed to ensure that the required repairs were made and they were carried out at the sole expense of Lord and Lady Barnard. Fordyce suggests that the actions of Lord Barnard had been instigated by his wife 'who was so strongly exasperated against her son that she attempted to set fire to the Castle'. Lord Barnard died in 1723, aged 70; his wife Elizabeth survived him only by two years.

Now Surtees himself takes up the story. In a letter to Sir Cuthbert Sharp, he tells that: 'This old jade, after her death, used to drive about in the air, in a black Coach and Six; sometimes she takes to the ground and drives slowly up the lawn to Alice's Well, and still more frequently walks the battlements of Raby, with a pair of brass knitting needles, and is called Old Hell Cat.'

Over the years those knitting needles have, we are told, been seen glowing red or even white hot amongst the battlements of Raby. Their colour may well depend upon the mood of the frenzied phantom herself while she looks out in envy across

Raby Castle gatehouse.

The lofty battlements, haunt of A'ad Hell Cat?

the great estate; once her own and so contemptuously passed down to her errant son. Or perhaps she simply looks on in enraged exasperation at the roof lead, which is still unstripped. As to the improbable location of the haunting, and to the even more curious accompaniment of knitting needles, the great Surtees is strangely silent.

⁂ RUTHALL RUED THE DAY ⁂

There is an old ecclesiastical saying which declares that 'York has the highest rack, but Durham has the deepest manger.' Obliquely phrased, this expression hints that although historically York may have been elevated to an archbishopric with greater ecclesiastical authority over Durham, the vast wealth generated from St Cuthbert's lands more than compensated the Prince Bishops of Durham for their nominal subordination to York. Throughout the medieval period, and indeed up until the prosaically entitled Municipal Corporations Act of 1835 prompted the demise of the Prince Bishops of Durham, Durham remained a very wealthy see and the prince bishop a very wealthy man.

Historically, the Prince Bishops of Durham counted amongst their number, as Sir Timothy Eden tells us, 'some of the most splendidly arrogant figures in English history'. They included a succession of warrior ecclesiastics; builders of castles, churches and, of course, Durham Cathedral; courtiers and confidantes to kings and queens; scholars; philanthropists; genuinely pious men; and the occasional rogue. Some spent vast portions of their wealth on personal projects, both philanthropic and self-aggrandising. But by the dawning of Tudor England, the great Warrior Bishops of Durham were a thing of the past. Royal patronage was now bestowed upon a new kind of prelate and bishops who held their office under King Henry VIII were required to have very different skills and talents.

Wealth, the accumulation of it and especially the keeping hold of it, was of considerable concern to Bishop Thomas Ruthall, who presided over his Durham Diocese between the years 1509 and 1523. He, as the Church histories have told us, saw the bishopric as 'a fount of riches, rather than as an independent principality'. Dean of Salisbury before becoming Bishop of Durham, Ruthall had an immense personal fortune. But the Church histories continued to be sparing in their flattery of him and the *Durham Diocesan History* published in 1881 notes little of interest during Ruthall's time in office.

Of course, at national level there was the Battle of Flodden, fought on 9 September 1513 at Branxton in Northumberland. It would be the last-ever battle fought between Scottish and English armies. Before the encounter the English commander, the Earl of Surrey, halted his army at Durham City in order to receive the sacred banner of St Cuthbert. It was to be carried into battle for the final time; the almost mystical talisman which had never flown above a defeated army.

Apart from this admittedly significant event, it is simply and perhaps tellingly recorded of Ruthall that 'nothing of interest is recorded of him in connection with the Diocese'. However, there was one curious thing for which Ruthall was remembered.

One day at Auckland Castle, Bishop Ruthall received a royal command from the king (sent via Henry's wily Lord Chancellor, Cardinal Wolsey), to prepare and forward to him a detailed survey and account of all Crown property, lands and revenues in the County Palatine of Durham. Ruthall was, of course, happy to do His Majesty's bidding. In fact, he would take the opportunity of such a survey to compile a record of his own wealth as prince bishop; a detailed account of his own splendid revenues.

In due course the task was completed but, upon examination of the respective inventories, Ruthall was alarmed to see that across his County Palatine lands the wealth generated for him as prince bishop far exceeded the wealth generated for the king himself. How might Henry react if he discovered that the bishop was the wealthier man? But equally, what might the king do if he wasn't told by Ruthall but subsequently found out? After some deliberation, Ruthall decided that silent discretion was the better policy and dutifully sent off the survey that had been prepared for Wolsey. He would now take some small pleasure in examining his own account, after judiciously saying nothing about it to the king. But the wrong document was sent to Henry.

Some have said that it must have been a simple, if unfortunate, accident since both documents had been bound in the same type of material. But however it had happened, accident, mistake or deliberately malicious act, what Wolsey received on the king's behalf was in fact a fully detailed account of the vast personal wealth of Thomas Ruthall in the Bishopric of Durham. It is said that Wolsey lost no time in telling Henry of his discovery and suggesting to the king that he now knew to whom he could turn if ever he was in need of money!

King Henry never did act to relieve the bishop of any of his fortune but when Ruthall, who had previously complained to Wolsey that the cost of maintaining his household of 300 retainers at Auckland Castle 'is the way to keepe a man poore', realised what had happened, he worried and fretted about what might happen next and gradually became so distressed that his health was affected. He quickly deteriorated and, on 4 February 1523, he died, leaving behind his vastly wealthy Diocese of Durham and an account to prove it.

The following year he was succeeded as Bishop of Durham by none other than Cardinal Wolsey, who apparently had given instructions for some 'particular, cinnamon scented rushes, which he considered alone, fit to be strewn on the floor of his bedchamber' to be planted in the grounds of Auckland Castle. For six years he benefited from the colossal income generated from St Cuthbert's lands. He eventually resigned, having never once visited his Diocese of Durham or sniffed his cinnamon-scented rushes.

⚜ SHARPE AND WALKER KILL'T THOU AND ME ⚜

In the mid-1600s, Henry More, in his work *The Immortality of the Soul*, argued that ghosts were then still effective 'in detecting the murderer, in disposing their estates, in rebuking injurious executors, in visiting and counselling their wives and children, in forewarning them of such courses, with other matters of like sort'.

In August 1631, probably the most curious trial ever to take place in the County Palatine of Durham was heard before Judge Davenport at the old Court of Assize on Palace Green in the shadow of the great cathedral.

It was a case, the bizarre nature of which would eventually be brought to the attention of no less an august body than the Royal Society. But it was a case that disturbed Judge Davenport greatly, that brought down upon him an intangible feeling of gloom and foreboding, and he was described by trial observers as a man 'who was very troubled'.

James Graham was a miller. He worked long, lonely hours at the Old Mill on the River Wear near Great Lumley. Of good standing and good reputation, he was also, so we are told by the *Monthly Chronicle*, 'A practical, no nonsense man, who would not court even an ignorant fear of the supernatural and who laughingly ridiculed all who thought different from himself'. This was until one dark night, when he was working alone in the mill.

The midnight hour had come and gone when Graham, suddenly disturbed, looked up from his work and saw moving towards him the figure of a rent and bloodied young woman, displaying five ghastly wounds. Graham, 'much affrighted and amaz'd, began to cross himself'. Then the terrible apparition spoke: 'I am the spirit of Anne Walker, who while in the flesh, lived with your neighbour John Walker; I was betrayed by Walker.' The ghost went on to tell the miller that Walker had paid another man, Mark Sharpe, a collier from Blackburn in Lancashire, to murder her and that Sharpe 'slew me with a pick, such as men dig coal withal, and gave me these five wounds'. The ghost instructed Graham to go and report what she had told him to the authorities.

John Walker of Great Lumley was a 'yeoman of good estate' and Anne Walker's uncle. Anne 'a pleasing young woman of about 25', had lived with him as his housekeeper. But recently she had not been seen. The story had been put about by Walker that she had been unwell and sent off, to stay for her recuperation, with an aunt in Chester-le-Street. The people of the village, however, suspected that the real reason for Anne's disappearance was the fact that Walker had got her pregnant. For Walker was not quite liked by the local population, he was 'scarcely respected; nobody could well say why they did not like him, but all felt a constraint in his company and a feeling that he was not right at the core'.

At first, because of the bizarre circumstances, Graham was reluctant to go to the authorities; after all he had his reputation and his business to protect. But twice more the ghost of Anne Walker appeared to him and made the same request. Soon the request became a demand and each time she was more alarming in aspect. In the second visitation she was 'Stern and Vindictive' and in the third 'Very fierce and cruel'. That was it. Graham finally went to the magistrate and repeated, word for word, the tale that the ghost of Anne Walker had told him.

A search was organised and the unfortunate girl's body found, bearing the terrible wounds previously witnessed by Graham and dumped in a pit at the exact location her ghost had described. A description which also led to the discovery of the murder weapon and the blood-soaked clothes of Mark Sharpe, hidden under a nearby bank: 'The pick and shoes and stockings, still bloody in every circumstance, as the apparition had related.' Sharpe and Walker were duly arrested and put on trial for murder. And, no doubt due to the seemingly uncanny nature of the case, the arrest created 'an immense sensation'.

This strangest of trials opened and was quickly over with Judge Davenport giving judgement on the first night, 'which was a thing never used in Durham, before nor after'. Indeed, the judge later wrote a letter describing his experiences during the trial: 'a very full and punctual narrative of the whole business.' No confessions were ever made, either by Sharpe or Walker, even though local gossip told that Sharpe had admitted Walker had paid him £10 to murder his niece.

More ghostly evidence was apparently revealed to the foreman of the jury at Walker's trial. Mr James Smart of Durham City later stated that the foreman (a Mr Fairhair of Ford, near Lanchester) gave evidence under oath attesting that while proceedings were taking place he witnessed, to his horror, 'the likeness of a child, stand upon Walker's shoulders'. This seemed definitive proof, if any more was needed, and the vision was regarded 'very fit and apposite, placed on Walker's shoulders, as the one who was justly loaded or charged with that crime of getting his kinswoman with child, as well as complotting with Sharpe to murder her'. Both Sharpe and Walker were duly found guilty and hanged at Durham.

What then is the modern-day reader to make of the case and of James Graham's evidence? Because his testimony (given to him by the ghost) led the authorities straight to the location of the body, the murder weapon and the other damning

The site of the curious trial of Sharpe and Walker.

evidence, then surely there are only three possibilities. Either what he reported was a true story, which would be, to say the least, unusual. Or did he or somebody known to him witness the murder? But why then concoct such a fantastic story? Alternatively, perhaps Graham himself was the killer; a scenario which was apparently never suspected or even considered at the time. Some 200 years later, however, his evidence may not have brought about the same conclusion.

In Southam, Warwickshire, a farmer was murdered. The next morning a man called on the farmer's widow, to tell her that the previous night her husband's ghost had appeared to him, showing him the fatal stab wounds and giving the name of the murderer and the location of the body. A search was made and the body found. The alleged murderer was arrested and brought for trial. The judge on this occasion said that he did not know of any law that admitted that a ghost could give evidence, and even if there was one, the ghost had not appeared in court to give it. However, being scrupulously fair, he asked the clerk of the court to call the ghost as a witness. This he did three times, but each time the ghost failed to appear. The accused man was duly acquitted and the judge ordered that the witness whose ghostly testimony had led to the wrongful arrest be detained on suspicion of being the actual murderer. Proof of his guilt was eventually obtained and he was executed at the next assizes.

❧ SILVER PENNIES IN HIS PURSE ❧

Whosoever looks up at this mass of masonry, may truly say; how terrible and tremendous is this place.

Such was the observation of Durham Cathedral, made by the Bishop of Ely in 1235.

Today, if you were to ask any of the cathedral stewards, 'where is the tightrope walker's grave?' they would, probably without hesitation, point to an ancient and much worn grave cover just outside the North Door. But as to whose grave it actually covers, mystery and legend speak of more than one possibility.

Sir William Brereton was a general of the Parliamentarian army during the English Civil War. However, seven years before that bloody conflict, as part of a tour he was making of County Durham, he had cause to visit Durham Cathedral, recording in his journal an old legend which was related to him on his visit.

Sir William was shown a stone grave cover and effigy near the North Door of the cathedral and was told that there lay the body of 'he who had been the Steward of the Purse, at the time of the Cathedral's building'; a man by the name of Hub a' Pella or Hob of Pelaw. It was the steward's task every day to distribute money, as payment for materials delivered or works completed in the course of the cathedral's construction. But Hob, it seems, had divine assistance. For it was reported to Sir William Brereton that even though, at the end of every day, the steward's purse would be empty, invariably the next morning it would be 'miraculously' replenished, filled again with coins ready for the new day's expenditure 'and by this means was the great work built'.

Over the centuries, falls from the cathedral's 'dizzying heights' have been many and usually, but not always, fatal. On 15 June 1829, a young man by the name of William Taylor, who was apprenticed to John Forsyth of Durham (a roofer and slater), was sent to make some repairs to the ceiling of the Chapel of the Nine Altars. Unfortunately, as he was doing so, he overbalanced. He plummeted the 78ft to the stone flags beneath but 'wonderful to relate, received only trifling injury'.

Not all, however, have been so fortunate. The next story involves the Prior of Durham, the King of England and an acrobat.

In 1237, following the death of the previous bishop, the Prior of Durham, Thomas Melsonby, was elected by the Durham monks to be their new bishop. However, his appointment was blocked by King Henry III, who succeeded in 'keeping him back from honour'. The king maintained that Melsonby was unfit to be Bishop of Durham and accused him, probably falsely, of 'breaking his vows, being an infringer of the liberties of the church, being diseased in body, being guilty of the misuse of church funds and selling church favours'. The king went on to claim that Melsonby was illiterate and of low birth, allegedly being the illegitimate son of the rector of Melsonby and his 'maid-servant'.

Of course, these were treacherous and dangerous times of plot and counterplot, when kings of England usually needed the unswerving and guaranteed support of the powerful bishops, and King Henry may have felt that Melsonby of Durham was simply unreliable. But a far more serious charge levelled by the king, against Melsonby, was that of murder.

This referred to an incident when, as an entertainment, Melsonby had arranged for an acrobat or tightrope walker, 'for payment of a purse of silver pennies', to exhibit his skills 'upon a chord, suspended from two towers of the church; from which height he fell and broke his neck'. The unfortunate man was buried in the grave, which is still known by his name and which some say bears his effigy, near the North Door of the cathedral, close to the spot where his body fell. Curiously, however, there is another story, which seems to challenge both of the former and most popular accounts.

In his *Local Records*, published in 1866, the chronicler John Sykes relates that in 1829 much of the churchyard on the north side of the cathedral was cleared of rubbish and levelled. During this work, 'many ancient tomb stones were revealed'. And it was at this time that it was discovered that the mysterious effigy near the North Door was in fact 'the effigy of Lady Lumley, who had been buried below'. Sykes goes on to tell us that, under a licence of Bishop Matthew given in the late sixteenth century, the then Lord Lumley received permission to remove the bones of his ancestors from their place of burial 'near the North Door of the church,

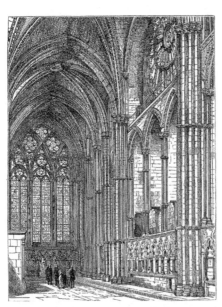

Chapel of the Nine Altars, Durham Cathedral, the scene of William Taylor's fall.

The western towers and North Door. The tightrope walker's grave is just in front of the door and to the left in the picture.

the very place in question'. However, the licence only gave permission for the removal of male ancestors, thus Lady Lumley remained where she lay.

So whose grave is it?

That of Hob of Pelaw, Steward of the Purse, who with due diligence and apparently divine assistance carried out his daily duties, paying for the work carried out in the construction of the cathedral? Or that of the lonely Lady Lumley who, as Sykes tells us, was so long ago separated from her male kin?

The unfortunate tightrope walker did not survive in life to be paid his silver pennies but there are some who would tell you that, on occasion, his fateful cathedral fall is re-enacted in ghostly fashion. A sudden crash alarms those inside the building, as of the unfortunate man's body being broken on the rooftops above. Then can be heard his slow, inexorable slide down toward his ultimate doom; faint cries of agony mingle with the dreadful sounds of his fingernails desperately scratching, frantically feeling for, but failing to find, some saving handhold. And then, the sudden silence, as the incorporeal body makes its final fall to the churchyard below.

The effigy on that ancient gravestone, regardless of who actually lies beneath it, is now worn by the weather and by the years. However, there are those who maintain that, if you examine it closely, the carved outline of a purse can still just be seen. And what's more, given the right light (or perhaps after a shower of rain), what seem to be silver pennies are revealed, glistening within it. Of course it could just be lichen, but lichen has never really made for a good story!

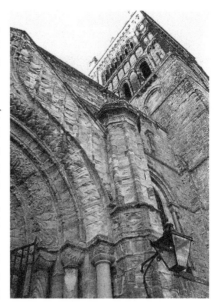

Dizzying heights.

The tightrope walker's grave, a much-eroded effigy.

❧ STICKS, STONES AND STAY BUSKS ❧

An anonymous contributor to the *Monthly Chronicle* of 1891 tells of a peculiar, archaic dialect, once commonly spoken by the shepherds of remote Weardale and particularly employed in the counting of their sheep. The numerals they used as part of this dialect, which 'differed from the common speech of the area', were of mysterious origin and in this strange tongue the numbers one to ten were transmogrified into 'yan, tean, tether, mether, pip, sezar, azar, catrah, horna, dik'. The contributor also noted that they seemed to share certain similarities with dialects spoken in the Yorkshire Dales and in Westmorland; perhaps not that surprising, given the relatively close geographical proximity of both regions. More surprising, however, is that our correspondent also drew comparisons with dialect numerals used by shepherds in the Welsh hills. He suggested that they perhaps shared a common ancestor in ancient Celtic speech, with even more distant linguistic roots in Hindustani, perhaps even Sanskrit.

The contributor went on to tell us that there may even have been a dialect connection across the Atlantic Ocean. An old gentleman from Hartford, Connecticut, had previously written that he had been taught, as a child, by an 'Old Indian Woman' who used to work at his father's house. Curiously, the numbers she had used when teaching the little American boy to count from one to ten bore a striking resemblance to those used in Weardale, and were these: 'een, teen, tudhur, fedhur, pip, sat, latta, poal, defri, dik.' However, our County Durham contributor went on to regret that 'civilisation is invading all the out of the way corners of the earth and all dialects and local distinctions are dying out' and he noted that, at the time of writing, 'extremely few people still use that language'.

Perhaps these archaic shepherd's numerals would have been known to Mr W.M. Egglestone of Stanhope, another contributor to the *Monthly Chronicle* and a collector of a number of Weardale's curiosities and trinkets. His discoveries hark back to an age long before the era of mass consumerism, an age when it was common practice for personal gifts or love tokens to be painstakingly crafted over many hours. Beauty and practicality were combined in the fine decoration of an everyday object which would be used over and over again, a permanent reminder of the affection with which it was given.

Knitting sticks were one such token. As to their function, that is self evident. Made usually of bone, they were shaped, carved and decorated by young men into ornamental presents for their sweethearts. They were, quite literally, a labour of love. Hours upon hours would be spent on their intricate decoration and, though they had no set pattern or design and each was as individual as its creator, there would often be carved into them the initials of the giver, or the recipient, or both, and perhaps the date of its presentation. The whole objective would be to make it as beautiful as possible. The accompanying sketch, we are told by

Knitting stick.

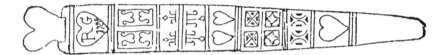

Stay busk.

Mr Egglestone, 'represents a good specimen', though he goes on, perhaps in a less romantic vane, to suggest that the actual carvings and designs of such pieces of work were: 'strikingly like those found on bows, quivers, knives, axes, clubs and other implements.'

A similar offering, given as a fancifully decorated love token (though perhaps of a more personal nature), was a carved stay busk; an article used for the stiffening and straightening of the bone corsets worn, or suffered by, the young ladies of eighteenth-century Weardale. Such a fine gift would no doubt be considered as being of special significance, assisting the recipient as it did, 'to make one of these (at the time) indispensible articles of dress', and the illustration shows an example of such 'an interesting relic of olden times'. Mr Egglestone informs us that the object, from which the illustration was made, was about 13in long by just over 1in broad, made of wood and dated, it was thought, to around the year 1728.

Holy stones, however, were definitely not love tokens and, at a time when the supernatural world was thought of as part of the everyday, they were probably considered to have far more serious significance. Otherwise known as hag stones, lucky stones, adder stones or witch stones, small examples would be worn or carried as personal amulets and their larger brethren placed as charms in a spot near the doors of houses to ward off evil. This practice, Mr Egglestone tells us, was once 'exceedingly common' in the dales of Northern England.

He goes on to inform us that the holy stone illustrated (on p. 126) was found by a farmer on the bed of a stream near St John's chapel around the year 1850, though its actual age was much older; and it was: 'highly valued as a charm against witchcraft and otherwise as a protection to the owner against evil spirits.' About 2in long and an inch thick, with a 'rude human face' carved into one side, there could still be seen on it the remains of a yellowish glaze, suggesting that at some

Holy stone.

time in the past it had been fired. There were also signs that that it had been broken, perhaps originally being part of 'a rudely formed idol'.

Of course, such rustic superstitions are now, probably, a thing of the past. Indeed, even in Mr Egglestone's time, he noted that the people of Weardale 'are getting more cultivated as years advance and are abandoning the fashions and habits of their forefathers'.

𝒯

⁕ THE TREASURES OF BISHOP MICHAEL ⁕

In 2009, there was a to-do in Durham City.

It was reported to the press by cathedral officials that over the course of a two-and-a-half-year licensed exploration of the River Wear around the peninsula, divers had brought up from the river bed a collection of hundreds of ancient artefacts, representing Durham's Roman, Anglo-Saxon and medieval past, all clearly of archaeological and historical significance. However, perhaps the most unusual finds were an odd collection, found mainly in the vicinity of Prebends Bridge, of over thirty unique and potentially very valuable pieces.

The story attracted local and national media attention after it was established that all of these objects had once belonged to Michael Ramsey (1904–88), formerly Bishop of Durham and Archbishop of Canterbury (the 100th incumbent of that office), who, after his retirement, had resided at a house in South Bailey. However, the objects in question were not his personal possessions but had been official gifts, received by him mainly during his time as archbishop. They included, as reported in the media, a silver trowel, presented to him in 1961 for laying the foundation stone of an Indian church; gold, silver and bronze medals, given to him in 1966 by Pope Paul VI commemorating the Second Vatican Council; a bronze icon from the head of the Russian Orthodox Church; a solid silver coin from the Greek Orthodox Church; and a solid gold coin from the leader of Japan's Buddhists. Also among the collection was a medallion commemorating the 1953 coronation of Queen Elizabeth II in which, as Bishop of Durham, he had taken part, supporting the right hand of the young monarch. It was estimated that the whole collection could be worth thousands, perhaps even tens of thousands of pounds. The question was, however, how had these precious items ended up on the bottom of the River Wear?

The possibility of simple theft was put forward and it was suggested that perhaps a burglary had taken place at his residence, only a few hundred yards away from Prebends Bridge, although no official report had ever been made to the police. Perhaps, it was thought, during their getaway, the thieves had realised that the objects they had taken were so unusual and recognisable (and therefore potentially difficult to offload) that they simply threw them off the bridge, into the river below. It was further suggested that, since by that time the old archbishop was becoming physically frailer and apparently more forgetful, he may not even have realised that the objects were gone.

However, the divers themselves pointed out that the items had been found in six different locations, only four of which were in the close vicinity of Prebends Bridge. All of the locations were easily accessible from the river banks, which led

Prebends Bridge.

Across Prebends Bridge, a popular walk.

them to believe that the objects had not simply been thrown from the bridge, but had actually been deliberately placed in the river at different locations and at different times. Perhaps by Dr Ramsey himself, who during his lifetime had gained a reputation for being something of an eccentric. Maybe he had placed the items there as a gesture, an odd kind of votive offering or even as a symbolic gift for all time; giving them 'to the river and to the people of Durham, whom he loved'.

A fellow clergyman and personal friend of Dr Ramsey suggested that the old man had always felt uneasy receiving objects of such obviously high value. On a previous occasion he had sold a number of pieces privately, giving the proceeds of the sale to the charity Christian Aid. However, some of the objects had reappeared on the open market, upsetting the original donors and causing embarrassment to Dr Ramsey. He therefore didn't know what to do with the rest of them. He didn't need them and he probably felt uncomfortable having them in his possession. The same commentator seemed to support the divers' speculation, saying that what they suggested was consistent with Ramsey's character: 'that's so Michael Ramsey!' This friend had visited Dr Ramsey and his wife every year, staying with them for a time at their house in South Bailey, and he confirmed that it was a habit of this 'brilliant but eccentric and unworldly' old man to, every day, regardless of the weather, take his walk around his beloved river banks. Perhaps Dr Ramsay was carrying on the ancient practice of making a personal offering to the *genius loci* (protective guardian spirit), as the divers seemed to suggest.

Interestingly, it is said of the nineteenth-century Durham historian Robert Surtees that he took to leaving small items of value in the pools, streams and little rivers around Mainsforth Hall as symbolic gifts to the countryside he loved. This may

of course be apocryphal, though Surtees certainly did love the rural scenes around his Mainsforth home and famously said that God had placed him in paradise.

In the end we may never know how those unique and valuable objects came to rest on the river bed in Durham City. But perhaps it is not such a great stretch of the imagination to consider that during his long association with Durham, Dr Ramsey could well have become familiar with the works of Robert Surtees. Moreover, if the stories of the somewhat unusual and eccentric ritual practises of the historian of Durham had become known to him, he may have found a practical and, for him, satisfactory solution to his own dilemma.

The approach to Prebends Bridge from South Bailey.

❧ THAT'S ENTERTAINMENT ❧

The citizens of Victorian Spennymoor were well served with theatrical drama. It was perhaps not always of the highest quality, but at least there was plenty of it.

In the early days, an evening's entertainment could be enjoyed at Collett's Booth, although the canvas roof – worn and holed – left the audience somewhat exposed to the elements. One winter night a young boy, somewhat bored, threw a snowball at the 'villain' as he made his entrance. The boy's aim was true and the enraged actor stopped mid-performance and said: 'I'll give half a crown to know who threw that!' As the audience seemed to think that this incident was actually the highlight of the evening's entertainment, the boy's identity was protected from thespian wrath.

In later years, the Cambridge Theatre was built, with a solid roof, though with scenery 'of a primitive description'. At one time, it was managed by a gentleman who always took the leading part in his own productions. He became very popular with the theatregoers, not only because of the nature of his plays, which were many and varied, but also for the way he swore, out loud, on stage, at his fellow actors, if he felt their performances were below par. He also accepted with good grace the customary heckling and verbal abuse hurled at him from the paying customers (the concept of audience participation is not a new one). One day, however, he announced with great solemnity the title of the gripping drama which he was to offer the following week; a particularly serious and thought-provoking production, appropriate no doubt for an audience which consisted mainly of coal miners and their families. Its title: *The Danger of the Mines.*

And so, on the first night, the audience came in their numbers and in great anticipation. The curtains opened. The 'primitive' and decidedly insubstantial scenery revealed the inside of a coal mine and smoky darkness filled the stage as the (very small) orchestra struck up a mournful air. Suddenly, through a hole in the ceiling, descended a large basket, dangling rather alarmingly by a single strand of rope. Slowly, unsteadily, with our hero's white knuckles clasped around the rope, the basket descended to the bottom of the imaginary shaft. Loud applause now rang out; the night was going well! Soon, as the star hewed with his pick at the painted coal seam, the miners were cheering him on and shouting instructions about how to do it better. With their roars of encouragement, our hero was swept away with his obvious success, and his hewing became a little too vigorous for the shaky scenery; the more he hewed, the more the scenery shook. The sound in the theatre grew to a cacophony. Suddenly, above all the noise, came an enormous crash and roll of a great drum! Our thespian miner had been caught in a pit explosion! As the drum boomed out, our hero flung himself across the stage as if blasted. At the same time, the much-hacked-at scenery toppled over and crashed down onto the stage. Gasps of astonishment came from the audience as the curtains were closed, leaving our hero, as Dodd suggests, doubtless 'struggling in the after-damp'.

❖ ULYSSES S. GRANT AND THE CODY BOYS ❖

Some readers may remember the 1977 visit of US President Jimmy Carter to Newcastle, Sunderland and Washington Old Hall. But this was not the first visit to the North East of England by a commander-in-chief. For, a hundred years before, County Durham had played host to the American president of those days.

Ulysses S. Grant was the great military hero of the republic during the American Civil War. Despite barely passing West Point Military Academy's height requirement for entrance, and eventually graduating a somewhat less than outstanding twenty-first out of his class of thirty-nine students, he went on to lead the Union Army as general-in-chief and be largely credited with defeating the Confederacy, accepting its surrender on 9 April 1865. Ten days later he would be a pallbearer at the funeral of Abraham Lincoln.

After the war he was elected 18th President of the United States. A somewhat larger-than-life character, he drank and smoked heavily, one story telling of him puffing his way through 10,000 cigars in five years. He also remains, for now at least, the only American president on record to be given a speeding ticket, which he received for running his horse and buggy too quickly through the streets of Washington DC. He would serve two terms as president, ending in March 1877. And, in the September of that same year, he was in Sunderland.

As part of his two-year world tour he came to the North East of England, where he was welcomed by the civic dignitaries of Newcastle, North Shields, Gateshead and Jarrow. On 24 September 1877, twelve years after accepting the surrender of General Robert E. Lee at Appomattox Court House, Virginia, he stood alongside the Mayor of Sunderland, Alderman Storey, at the laying of a commemorative stone on the foundations of Sunderland's new museum and library in Mowbray Park.

But Grant wasn't the only larger-than-life character to leave the shores of the New World and visit the old County Palatine of Durham. Another very familiar name from the Wild West was the showman supreme, William Frederick 'Buffalo Bill' Cody. Originally an army scout, he'd earned his nickname after allegedly killing 5,000 buffalo in eighteen months, for a contract to supply meat to the workers on the Kansas Pacific Railway. From 1883, he'd toured with his Wild West Show, with several lengthy stays in the UK. But in April 1904, appeared the following notice:

> Positively the last and final farewell tour of England, Wales and Scotland, by Buffalo Bill's Wild West and Congress of Rough Riders of the World.

This was indeed to be the final tour. It would include 132 towns and cities, from Cornwall to Inverness, a distance of 4,114 miles by train and another 441 miles just travelling from railway sidings to showgrounds and back. Most were one-day events, although sometimes they would stay two. Occasionally the booking would be for a week, as it was in Newcastle. The show, dubbed America's National Entertainment, was pulled by Barnum & Bailey Circus railway cars, with three trains pulling 150 carriages. The excitement would often begin with the participants, the 'Rough Riders of the World', riding their horses through the streets, waving at the assembled crowd, with Buffalo Bill Cody always at the very front of the procession.

So it was that throughout the month of July 1904, and for the final time, the citizens of County Durham, whether in Durham City or Darlington, Sunderland or Stockton, South Shields or West Hartlepool, joined those of Middlesbrough, Newcastle and North Shields in being amazed at the exploits of Buffalo Bill's Wild West and Congress of Rough Riders of the World. They no doubt looked on, open mouthed, at the recreation of the Battle of the Little Big Horn, starring Young Sitting Bull, a son of the famous Lakota Sioux chief who had led the 8,000-strong Sioux and Cheyenne force at the real battle and had been victorious over General George Armstrong Custer and his 7th Cavalry. The shows were massively popular. When they appeared in Sunderland, tram receipts went up by £238 in a two-day period with people travelling to see them. In Newcastle, over six days, receipts were £600 in excess of any other six days in the Corporation's history.

But Cody's moneymaking enterprises now lay more with his American mining interests and he was to leave the UK for good. That day finally came at Stoke-on-Trent on Friday, 21 October 1904, with, as the *Staffordshire Sentinel* proclaimed with great finality: 'Positively the last two performances of Buffalo Bill's Wild West in England – EVER!!'

But before Grant and Cody, another American, the great showman Phineas T. Barnum, had also been no stranger to the North East. Barnum crossed the Atlantic nearly forty different times, with attractions such as his Greatest Show on Earth. And in 1858, crowds gathered to hear his lecture on 'The Art of Money Getting'. In April the following year, he was back again. The attendees expected more amusing anecdotes about, and advice on, the use of trickery and deceit as a means to part gullible customers from their money. They were surprised, and no doubt more than a little disappointed, therefore, when Barnum, the Apostle of Humbug, proceeded to lecture them on the importance of punctuality, perseverance, strict accuracy in accounting and economy, as the essentials of success.

'Amuse the public by all means,' he told them, 'but educate them, and help them to be better men and women at the same time.'

But at least this sober and serious lecture ended on a lighter note, with the exhibition of the Feejee Mermaid, who, wrote a contributor to the *Monthly Chronicle*, 'while hideous, was a curiosity worth seeing'.

When his ship sailed from Liverpool at the end of October 1904, Buffalo Bill Cody, his cowboys and Indians, his sharpshooters and his mock battles, were gone for good. Seven years later, however, the residents of Brandon (about 3 miles from Durham City) were convinced that he'd returned. But it seemed to them that the great showman had surpassed even his most spectacular entertainment extravaganzas of previous years, for this time he'd dropped in on the village from the sky. In a flying machine.

Phineas T. Barnum.

When a stricken aircraft was seen making a forced landing, alarmed and curious villagers rushed to the scene. A lone figure emerged from the debris of broken struts and torn wing coverings. When asked his name, the stranger replied, in a clear American accent, 'Cody'. Could it really be him? The stranger did look very much like the great showman himself: the goatee beard was there, the leather boots. Clearly Buffalo Bill was back!

But he wasn't!

For this was Samuel Franklin Cody, showman, pioneer aviator and kite enthusiast. Born Franklin Cowdery, in Davenport, Iowa around 1867, as a youth he had become a real-life cowboy, herding and trailing cattle. When older he changed his name to Cody and developed a Wild West act, with sharpshooting tricks and horse-riding skills, reminiscent of Buffalo Bill himself.

The pair also bore a close physical resemblance and Samuel Franklin, playing to the image, with shoulder length hair, beard and moustache and donning Buckskins, cowboy boots and a Stetson hat, 'did nothing to dispel the public's confusion'. However, when he took his act to Europe in 1890, and actually claimed to be the son of the great showman (though in reality being no relation at all), he was promptly sued by Buffalo Bill.

Sam Cody arrived in England in 1903, only a year before Buffalo Bill's own final tour. But the entertainment he was offering the public had by now all been seen before and on a much bigger scale, meaning that his Wild West Show was not a success. So he turned, as a means of making money, to another great interest of his: making kites. Big kites. Man-lifting kites. He claimed to have been taught the skills of kite making and kite flying by Chinese cooks on the cattle trails of his youth and his aim was to develop his own design which could be used for military observation purposes, in preference to the hot-air balloons used at the time.

Initially he received backing from a keen British military and Cody now devoted all his time to aviation, working at Farnborough. Gradually, his kites became more and more sophisticated, and he eventually attempted to add engines to them, but soon his attention was turned to true powered flight in embryonic aircraft. In 1908 he was successful in his endeavours and, on 16 October of that year, his own bamboo and canvas flying machine took off to a height of about 20ft, flew above the ground for about thirty seconds at 25 miles an hour and, after covering a distance of 1,390ft, crashed. But Cody had done it. It was officially recorded as the first powered flight in Britain.

Unfortunately for him, in the rush for aviation development, other, younger, engineers were beginning to design more advanced aircraft than his own and he eventually lost military backing and military money. He would have to finance any further developments from his own pocket and he noted drily: 'The limit of my success, however, is bound by the limit of my capital.' His main income would now be from prize money, won in flying races. In 1910, he won the prestigious Michelin Cup and in the same year, in a different aircraft, he finished fourth in the Round England Race. And this is how he came to Brandon. He crash landed on 25 July 1911, during an air race.

His broken biplane attracted a host of sightseers; some probably still convinced that they were in the presence of Buffalo Bill. For two days he stayed whilst, with the invaluable assistance of two local milliners, Eva and Bessie Hornsby, repairs were made to the damaged sailcloth wing coverings. With the repairs complete, Cody rejoined the air race and finished second.

Samuel Franklin Cody was killed on 7 August 1913 when, during a pleasure flight over Laffan's Plain, Farnborough, his aircraft broke in half at 500ft. At his funeral, during which his coffin was carried on a gun carriage drawn by six black horses, an estimated crowd of 100,000 lined the route and he was buried in Aldershot Military Cemetery with full military honours.

So it was not the legendary Buffalo Bill Cody that crash-landed at Brandon in 1911, but if the locals were at all disappointed, they need not have been. For the magnificent man with his flying machine that descended upon them that day, Samuel Franklin Cody, was a character equally larger than life.

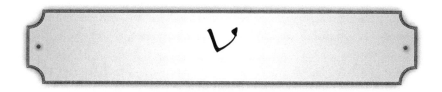

⁜ VICAR SKELLY'S WILL ⁜

In the eighteenth century, epitaphs, written in verse upon headstones, were very popular. Indeed, a small selection has been included in this book already. But it seems that fondness for such poetry was not exclusive to headstones and the writers of wills and testaments were also given to verse.

The illustration shown is said to represent the Revd John Ellison, sitting with his lawyer, who is drawing up the vicar's will. Ellison was, for fifty-four years, the vicar of Bedlington in Northumberland and, for forty-one years, the curate of St Andrew's church in Newcastle. During his lifetime Ellison was also, however, the victim of a distressing imposture. An anonymous writer, in a pamphlet entitled 'Parson Jock's Will', published a copy of what purported to be the

The Vicar's Will.

Last Will and Testament of the Revd Ellison in which, over seven verses of coarse, defamatory rhyme he 'discharged copious venom' at prominent local individuals of the day. The good parson was of course totally innocent of the outrage but of the real writer, and the reasons for his invective verse, 'who he was, has never been ascertained'.

The Revd John Skelly was vicar of Stockton-on-Tees between 1742 and 1772 and was a contemporary of Ellison. Vicar Skelly's will, in contrast, contained neither coarseness nor invective and was definitely his own verse. And, no doubt because of its humorous and slightly self-mocking nature, it was thought curious enough by the Revd John Brewster to print it on the flyleaf of a copy of his work *The Parochial History and Antiquities of Stockton-upon-Tees*. It reads as follows:

> What, Morgan dead! Upon my life,
> We have another chance, my wife;
> And as, my dear, they die so soon,
> I'll make my will this afternoon;
> To four good men give each a daughter,
> To Dr Riddal my cask of porter;
> My hat and wig won't do for a beau,
> But'll do very well to fright the crows;
> My gown and band to some old parson,
> My tything block to good friend Lawson,
> My boots and spurs put up to lot,
> Who gets my snuffy coat? A Scot,
> For there he'll forage for a year;
> So let it not be brushed, my dear.
> My shoes to John, I've but two pair,
> To old Will Wright pray give my mare.
> I'll keep this will in case I live;
> I may perhaps have more to give,
> Which shall be added when I've time;
> And can compose another rhyme;
> Sign'd, sealed, published, witnessed three,
> My wife, my daughter Bess, and me.

Incidentally, Vicar Skelly was also famous in his time for being instrumental in putting a stop to 'the inhuman custom of throwing at cocks on Shrove Tuesday'. This ancient blood sport necessitated a cockerel being tied to a post, after which participants would take turns in throwing a specially weighted stick – a cockstele – at the unfortunate bird until it was eventually killed.

The custom, described by Samuel Pepys as being, in his day, 'of considerable antiquity' had apparently been enjoyed, perhaps surprisingly, by Sir Thomas More, who supposedly showed some skill at it as a boy. It may originally have been symbolic of national enmity against the French and it was included by William Hogarth in his series of engravings entitled *The Four Stages of Cruelty*.

❖ VISIONS IN THE SKY ❖

In his book *County Durham*, Sir Timothy Eden makes an oblique reference to a phenomenon, allegedly witnessed in the skies over County Durham towards the end of the eighteenth century, which was curiously out of place in the old County Palatine.

Over the centuries, sightings of alleged phantom armies have been reported many times, with probably the most famous and repeated instance occurring at least three times on Midsummer Eve, between 1735 and 1745, at Souther Fell in Cumbria. Columns of red-coated troops were seen apparently crossing the fell high up near the summit, filling the space of about half a mile. They were led by mounted officers and trailed baggage wagons and powder-tumbrils. In reality, the terrain that they appeared to be crossing was so precipitous and rough (falling away sharply in steep slopes to either side of them) that they could not possibly have physically been there. They made no noise or sound of marching and, on later investigation by witnesses, had left behind no evidence of their passing. Statements attesting to the truth of the events were afterwards signed by witnesses.

Less famous incidents included the occurrence, in 1750, of a vanishing army, witnessed in Glen Aray, Scotland. And a century before that there were two alarming incidents in Aberdeenshire. The first involved an army witnessed marching in formation out of the morning mist, before simply vanishing in the sunlight; the second, a phantom battle, which seemed so real to those watching that some even hurriedly buried their personal belongings for safe keeping.

Ghostly armies and their spectral battles have also been seen in the skies. Around Christmas time 1642, the aerial replay of the English Civil War Battle of Edge Hill was well documented as witnesses watched over several nights, seeing the battle fought again and again in the sky and even recognising combatants known to them who had fallen on the field of conflict. On 10 July 1758, in the skies around Inveraray Castle, five witnesses in two different locations watched a battle between soldiers from what was clearly, by their dress, a Highland regiment, attacking a position defended by men in what looked like French uniforms. Bizarrely, this seemed to be a vision of a real event which had happened in America, when 300 Highlanders were killed assaulting a French fort.

And County Durham was to share in these weird aerial spectaculars, as Sir Timothy Eden tells us:'soon portents of prodigious events would be witnessed in the Durham skies; and the French Revolution would fall like a knife on the white neck of Beauty.' So it was that astonished witnesses in County Durham were destined to see, fighting in the sky, not British Redcoats, or Highland regiments, or soldiers of the English Civil War, but, apparently, combatants in the French Revolution.

The *Monthly Chronicle* of 1891 gives the following account:

> Aerial armies are declared to have been observed in the county of Durham towards the end
> of the last century. Myriads of fighting men, it is said, were seen in the sky, night after night,
> all through the County, before the French Revolution. Indeed, some people averred that they
> had distinctly heard the cries of the combatants and the groans of the wounded!

Curiously, in 1840 and again in 1857, a phantom island appeared in the sky off the island of Sanday, Orkney. It remained visible for most of the day and witnesses reported that it seemed covered in white buildings. Some were content with the more romantic explanation that what they were witnessing was a fairy isle. Others, more prosaically but perhaps more realistically, asserted that the vision was probably a mirage of part of the Norwegian coastline; perhaps something akin to the fabled, if natural mirage phenomenon, of the Fata Morgana.

So do such visions owe their explanation to a natural phenomenon, perhaps, as the *Monthly Chronicle* proposes, some kind of 'Atmospheric Refraction' bringing about a ghostly illusion of some real scene or actual event happening elsewhere? Interestingly, most of the mid-eighteenth-century sightings of Redcoats occurred before the time of the Jacobite uprising of Charles Edward Stuart (Bonnie Prince Charlie) and therefore before the troop movements of that particular conflict were a military reality. Perhaps they were intended, as Sir Timothy Eden seems to suggest, as a form of warning about the coming violence and turmoil.

Nothing can really explain why these fighters of the French Revolution were seen in the skies of County Durham, however. And, as for the actual veracity and significance of these apparently alarming events, that must remain for the reader to consider.

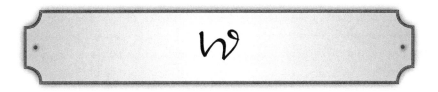

❧ WANDERING WILLIE ❧

This is a bit of a shaggy dog story. But the dog in question became something of a local hero, 'celebrated on the Shields ferry by its devoted and persevering search for its master'.

In August 1873, a shepherd from the Cheviot Hills in Northumberland, ably assisted as always by his working dogs, set out south on a long drove to the Cleveland Hills. On reaching the River Tyne, shepherd, sheep and sheepdogs boarded the steam ferry and crossed into South Shields for their onward journey through the County Palatine. The crossing went well and all were safely disembarked on the quayside. The sheep, however, being naturally accustomed to their native high open spaces, were soon startled and thrown into confusion by the noisy, thronging streets. They bolted and 'in astonishment and consternation', fled in all directions and were scattered. But the dogs were immediately sent to retrieve them and soon the sheep were once again gathered back together. After a quick count, however, the shepherd found that one of his sheep was still missing. So it was that he sent his best, most trusted and most faithful dog to retrieve that single errant sheep. Off the dog went to search street after crowded street.

However, as fate would have it, after a recount of his flock, the relieved shepherd realised that he'd made a mistake and that all of his sheep were present. So, as time pressed, he decided to move off on his southward journey, confident that his dog would catch up with him. But the dog never did. It returned, hours later, to the same spot on the quayside and lay down exhausted, there to wait for the return of its absent master. And there he waited. And waited. He waited for day after day, until days turned into weeks and then into months. And his master never came back.

The local people tried to befriend the dog but he would have none of it. He left uneaten the food offered by kindly souls and backed away suspiciously when approached, waiting always for his lost master to return: 'he would enlist under no other leader, in the place of him whom he had followed from the hills.' He eventually even took to travelling back and forth across the river on the ferry. And so it was for six months, with the dog surviving by scavenging scraps along the quayside 'and so providing for his own maintenance'.

Eventually the dog's health began to wane, though his resolve remained as strong as ever. Thrown overboard from the ferry by some uncharitable soul he survived and, just a week later, was back at his usual spot on the quayside and back on the ferry. A year went by and at last the drover returned. After making enquiries about his dog and hearing of its lonely wait, he set about looking for it. Up and down the quayside he searched but again, as fate would have it, on this day of all days, the dog was absent. Once again time pressed, the shepherd couldn't tarry and so reluctantly he boarded the ferry, leaving the dog behind and resigned to the fact that he 'could not recover him on that journey'.

Eventually, Willie, as the dog was locally christened, began to allow people to befriend him, even to take him into their homes, 'for he had awakened the widest sympathy by his devotion'. He would perhaps even stay with them for a couple of weeks or so, before invariably returning to the quayside and the ferry, to resume his vigil. However, more concerns were raised about him at the end of 1874. Many thought he would not survive the winter, for he was thin and gaunt, 'a mere ruckle of bones'. But Willie did survive, largely due to the kindness of the people who knew him, and it was said that 'he was even seen at last to wag his tail'.

Time went on. Willie eventually regained his strength and renewed his search for his now long-gone master. By now he had become an object of much interest and affection and, at last willing to accept the often copious offerings of food brought to him, he grew fat. Willie developed a bond with the ferryman, who became his unofficial keeper, and he became a well-known and much-loved attraction on the ferry. On alighting on either bank of the river, Willie would be the first off the boat, barking furiously as if it were 'a proclamation that he had brought all the passengers safely across the water'. And this he continued to do for several years until eventually, the novelty wore off.

For Willie had also been befriended by the hordes of local urchins who, 'turning to mirth all things on earth, as only boyhood can, joined chorus with Willie, and created such a nuisance that the poor brute and his ragamuffin comrades had to be banished from the locality of the landing places', the very places where, for years, the faithful dog had carried out his lonely and fruitless vigil. It was the beginning of the end for Willie. The dog began to grow disconsolate, his indomitable spirit finally seemed broken and Willie, with his keeper, Ralph the ferryman, 'was afterwards but occasionally seen in the streets of Shields'. So it was that time eventually caught up with the ever-faithful dog. He gradually became blind and infirm before at last, in 1880, 'old age finished his career'.

Wandering Willie, after his years of devotion and celebrity, had come to his natural end. But not for this ever-faithful dog the lasting fame of Edinburgh's Greyfriars Bobby. No statue in his image was ever commissioned by the civic worthies of South Shields, but rather, something much more prosaic. For the account of his adventures ends by telling us that Ralph the ferryman 'had him

Wandering Willie.

stuffed, placed in a glass case and exhibited in the Sunderland Museum', from where, we are assured: 'Many thousands, attracted to the exhibitions, have gazed on this memorial of animal fidelity.'

⁖ WHO TOLLED THE CURFEW BELL? ⁖

In medieval times, the curfew bell rang out every night across Durham City. Every night a bell-ringer would climb the bell tower steps and, just before nine o'clock, would toll the curfew. Every night the bell spoke out in a familiar language; a language which gave a voice to the collective fears and memories of terrifying Scots raids in years gone by. It spoke loud across the old city and told its citizens to dowse all fires and dim all lights. But one Saturday night, something happened which meant that the curfew bell would never again be tolled on that particular day of the week.

There have been, over the years, a number of different explanations for this state of affairs. One of them claims that soldiers on duty one Saturday night, whilst guarding the Scottish prisoners held in the cathedral after the Battle of Dunbar in 1650, got drunk and forgot to ring the curfew bell. But why the bell was not simply rung again the next Saturday night is unclear. Another, more sinister explanation is given in the form of a curious tale.

One Saturday night many years ago, witnesses on Palace Green saw the bell-ringer running frantically, breathlessly, towards the cathedral. He was late. Whatever attractions had preoccupied him, it was likely that they had caused him to fail in his civic duty, and for that, it was likely that he would have to suffer some form of punishment. Whatever this punishment was, it was obviously something he feared and witnesses claimed to have heard him gasp the words: 'The Devil take me, if I don't ring the Curfew Bell'. In what seemed like no time, he burst through the great North Door of the cathedral and clattered up the steps to the bell tower. All, it seemed, was well; the curfew bell was rung. Curiously, however, the bell-ringer did not reappear.

The curfew bell rang out across the city.

The alarm was soon raised after he had failed to return from the tower. A search was made but he was nowhere to be found. He was not in the bell chamber, nor on the tower steps, nor indeed was he anywhere inside the great cathedral. Had he somehow fallen from the tower? Again a search was made, this time around the outside of the building, and again, nothing; no bell-ringer, no body. The man had simply vanished as if spirited away. When the words that he had been heard breathlessly uttering were reported, there was an uneasy and unspoken feeling of alarm. What had happened to him? Where had he gone? After all, the curfew bell had been rung; if not by him, then by whom, or what? Be careful what you wish for!

Who tolled the curfew bell?

The bell-ringer was never seen again and no trace of him was ever found!

So it was that, from that day on, none would dare ascend the bell tower on a Saturday night for fear of any dread thing that may manifest itself in those dark, lofty and lonely recesses. Never more, on that day of the week, would the curfew bell ring out across the old city.

Many years later this story came to the attention of two young girls, one of them the daughter of the Archdeacon of Durham. And, with a commendable spirit of adventure and daring, they determined to conceal themselves in the cathedral one Saturday night in order to see what they might discover. At first they wandered around, innocently enough, before concealing themselves beneath a pew, waiting until they could bravely ascend the feared bell tower steps. Soon the vigilant vergers cleared the cathedral of people. The great doors boomed shut and the sound of keys turning in locks echoed through the empty massiveness of the building. Utter silence fell. Total darkness descended and embraced the two young adventurers.

Sometime later, frantic screams were heard coming from the cathedral. As would-be rescuers reached the North Door, they heard small fists beating frantically upon great timbers. Terrified and breathless, the girls were retrieved from the darkness, much the worse for their experience. What had they seen? What had they feared? All that the chronicles tell us, somewhat cryptically, is that, to those two girls: 'did not fall the glory of discovering why the Curfew Bell had not been tolled since that fateful night long ago'.

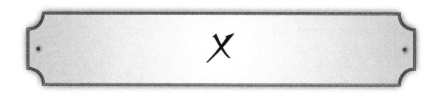

✤ X MARKS THE SPOT! – OR DOES IT? ✤

On January 30, 1756, a pot was found with 142 pieces of Scots silver coin, about 300 years old, in the grounds of Burn Hall, near Croxdale.

So we are told by Mackenzie and Ross, writing in 1834.

We all remember childhood tales of pirates on the high seas, treasure hoards and, of course, secret maps on which, invariably, an X shows the position of a buried fortune. Today, metal detectorists regularly turn up items left behind or lost by people long ago but the classic image of buried treasure, of locked chests full to bursting with gold and jewels, belongs mainly to the world of make-believe. Mainly that is, but not always.

Nationally of course there has, over the years, been a number of significant finds. Hoards, precious both in value and in historical significance, have been left behind by Romans, Saxons and Vikings. But treasure comes in different forms and, scattered around County Durham, a range of items with some dating from previous centuries and some indeed from previous millennia have been found. From the Late Bronze Age hoard of Heathery Burn Cave, near Stanhope, which was found in the mid-nineteenth century and which now resides in the British Museum, to the 'fine gold Nero, found by a woman hoeing turnips on Gillygate Moor'. From the exquisite sixth-century Anglo-Saxon glass beaker, discovered in 1776 at Castle Eden and regarded by the British Museum as 'probably the finest and most perfect specimen of Saxon grave glass in the country', to the twelve coins from the reign of King Ecgfrith of Northumbria (unearthed in Heworth churchyard and dated from the years AD 670 to AD 685 they are the earliest known coins of Northumbria and the only examples of their kind). And from a fourteenth-century knight's gold gauntlet ring, found near Durham City and possibly lost by a participant in the Battle of Neville's Cross, to the hundreds of votive offerings found by divers in the River Tees, at Piercebridge. Who knows what else may lie buried under the soil of County Durham!

No doubt most finds bring with them a degree of personal satisfaction and a sense of wonder. Some can be financially very lucrative, both for the finder and for the landowner, and on rare occasions a chance discovery can be life changing.

Early in the nineteenth century, Jackie and Nannie Taylor worked a large farm near Catchgate. They had a growing family to support and their life was hard. One day, Jackie was ploughing a field in particularly wet and difficult conditions. While Jackie pushed and urged on his labouring plough horses, Nannie walked in front, pulling. Suddenly the plough snagged on something buried in the ground. Jackie pushed harder, Nannie pulled harder and the two horses struggled harder until eventually they heard the sound of something smashing open. They quickly saw it was a large pottery vessel, obviously of some antiquity, and to their amazement they found that it was filled with old golden guineas. Whoever had left it there, and their reasons for leaving it, were lost in time but Jackie, being shrewd, sent the coins off to a 'trusted friend' in London, who changed them into the 'current coin of the realm' and returned that coin to Jackie. The story goes that following their find, Jackie and Nannie Taylor 'never looked back'. Jackie sold up and then bought another two farms, as well as a number of other properties. Eventually settling at Holmside, they lived in comfort for the rest of their days.

The good fortune of Jackie and Nannie Taylor was, we are told by the chroniclers, a matter of fact. But legends also tend to figure largely in treasure tales; as do dreams, it seems.

In the precincts of the old Roman fort at Ebchester, so a local legend told, was a cave, in which was secreted a treasure chest surmounted by a stylised guardian figure of, rather curiously, an ornamental crow. The chest, so it was said, was filled with treasure left behind by the Romans when they deserted Britain in the early fifth century. In the 1820s, an old man who lived at Ebchester began having a recurring dream about the legendary treasure and he set out to find it. To this end he actually began to 'sink shafts' in the vicinity of the fort. But, as the chronicler J.W. Fawcett tells us, 'success however, did not crown his efforts' and the old man was forced to desist 'more through exhaustion than failing faith'. Joshua Lax, a poet from Ebchester, alluded in one of his poems to the misadventure of the old treasure seeker:

> He worked hard for weeks the treasure to explore,
> But neither gold nor crow, to light could e'er restore.

A similar legend related to Friarside chapel, near Rowland's Gill. Standing secluded, roofless and ruined, it was said that 'untold wealth' was buried somewhere within its weed-strewn precincts and by the middle of the nineteenth century a number of attempts had been made to find it. At Winlaton Mill, John Heppell began to be plagued by repeated dreams of buried treasure; dreams that took him back, time and time again, to the ruined chapel of Friarside. The more he dreamt the same dream, the more he became convinced that the treasure did lie buried there, somewhere, just waiting to be found. And he determined to find it.

Confiding in a trusted friend, the two set out one night on their secret mission and, on reaching the chapel, began to dig a large hole at the western end. After a long night's digging, they had found nothing. Agreeing to return the following night, the pair set out for home. Unfortunately, on leaving the chapel, there appeared a mutual acquaintance, who, perhaps unsurprisingly, asked what they were doing. Their secret, it seemed, was out. They quickly needed some kind of explanation for their nocturnal activities and for the large hole in the ground which had obviously only recently been dug; something to divert attention away from the fact that they were actually looking for the legendary treasure of Friarside chapel.

To this end the story was proposed that they had just discovered the curious excavation and they thought that it must in fact be a grave, probably dug by murderers, to take the body of a would-be victim. This of course was a very curious state of affairs and unfortunately for the two treasure hunters, the story had exactly the opposite effect to that which they intended. Far from being a satisfactory, perhaps even a cautionary explanation to deflect any unwanted interest in the site and discourage casual visitors, the following day large numbers of curious onlookers descended on the scene of Heppell's secret nocturnal explorations, to witness for themselves the dastardly work of the supposed murderers. Indeed, this singular occurrence also attracted the attention of the authorities, the local newspapers and subsequently even some of the London journals. Needless to say, John Heppell's hopes of secretly finding the treasure of Friarside chapel were dashed for good and the mysterious hole, now the focus of keen public curiosity, was hastily filled in before, as they thought, being filled up by the body of some unfortunate victim of a heinous crime.

Of course, legendary stories of lost or hidden treasure have always, and probably will always 'readily give wings to the imagination and the fancies of men'. But the reality is that most treasure discovered today is found through educated guesswork or by pure chance. For treasure maps do not exist, legendary tales are mostly no more than that and X never marks the spot.

❧ YELLOWLY'S RECOLLECTIONS OF LION TAMERS ❧

Long before the days of the big top and the popular circuses of the twentieth century with their clowns, their acrobats and of course with their (now long gone) performing animals, travelling showmen toured the land with small collections of exotic beasts to the great astonishment of the populace. In 1732, a selection of wild beasts was brought to the North East. And the public wondered at a tiger, a leopard, a panther and a range of never-before-seen exotic birds. Six years later, the main attraction was a great camel.

It must be said, however, that the pedigree of some of these specimens and attractions was dubious to say the least. In 1750 came the visit of an 'Enterprising Exhibitor' who included in his collection a mummy, a porpoise and a mermaid, 'the two latter, alive'. A Victorian chronicler was later moved to comment that: 'What creature it was, a man or fish, that passed for a mermaid in the middle of the last century, the researches of the most patient local historian would hardly suffice to decide.'

Eventually, small exhibitions of curiosities and of strange, exotic or dangerous animals developed into travelling menageries. In the 1770s came 'The Wild Beasts; a noble collection of living, extraordinary productions', which, patrons were told, would be 'for the inspection of the curious only a few days, before proceeding to Sunderland'. And in 1799, a fantastical attraction, 'A stupendous elephant, the largest ever seen in Great Britain', came as part of Pidcock's Menagerie and was colourfully advertised as 'The Wonder of the Patrons of Pidcock'.

By the mid-nineteenth century, travelling menageries had become fully fledged entertainment shows and Hilton and Wright's wild beast shows were popular across the North East. Hilton's uncle lived at South Shields 'where he was popularly known as Baron Hilton' and he claimed to be the rightful heir to the Hylton Castle estates 'for the recovery of which, he entered an action at law'.

His show had no lions or tigers, but did include 'a magnificent jaguar from South America' and 'a good selection of lesser carnivorous and herbivorous beasts'. Novelty items were also included and people marvelled at a large Siberian wolf, which was confined in the same den as a sheep, above which was an inscription, painted in large letters: 'The Scriptures fulfilled: The wolf shall lie down with the lamb.'

William Yellowly of South Shields was fond of travelling collections. A naturalist and enthusiastic taxidermist, he doubtlessly had a more particular interest in their animal attractions and certainly one of his chief delights was George Wombwell's Monster Menageries.

George Wombwell had started life as a shoemaker, but a childhood fascination with birds and beasts had led him first to become a collector and then an exhibitor, gradually building up his collection before becoming a regular showman and 'amassing a handsome independence'. Assisted by his wife and an assortment of relatives, Wombwell's Menagerie became famous across the land.

Indeed, his caravan of wild beasts was so huge that it was divided into three different shows, 'each sufficiently extensive to excite wonderment'. The public loved them and they were such a great attraction throughout the North East, appearing regularly at fairs, race meetings and on public holidays, that it was said of these occasions: 'Wombwell's Menagerie, if absent, would have been felt as a blighted blank.' Darlington and Durham City were on their regular route and almost every year they over-wintered in the region. Yellowly himself described: 'A rare treat to see fifteen or sixteen large yellow caravans drawn into Shields market place by fifty or sixty powerful horses. The rhinoceros wagon alone being drawn by six splendid greys.' But William Yellowly was fascinated, not just by the animals and the acts but also by the resident lion tamers, their dangerous exploits and their seemingly exotic and glamorous lifestyle.

Manders' Menagerie was the chief rival of Wombwell's. On one visit to South Shields, posters were put up around the town advertising an amazing new attraction: an African tribal chieftain by the name of Macomo, who was advertised

Mr. George Wombwell   Mrs Wombwell

as 'The Greatest of Lion Hunters'. Yellowly it seems, was suitably impressed and gave a vivid description of the impression made by this mysterious chieftain:

> A dashing, athletic young fellow, with skin as black as ebony, and when seen in full war paint, with head dress mounted with the gorgeous feathers of the Blue and Scarlet Macaw, and his brawny arms and shoulders decorated with numerous strings of coloured beads and cowrie shells, he looked every inch a warrior.

But Macomo was in fact an African sailor, who Manders had hired in Liverpool, and he knew nothing about dangerous animals or their unpredictable behaviour. Clearly, this did not bode well for his future career in lion taming. Indeed, his time working for Manders would be blighted by injury, having a number narrow escapes and, perhaps unsurprisingly, being badly wounded on more than one occasion. And in 1868, whilst at Sunderland, there unfolded 'a scene of considerable alarm and excitement'. The lion he was working with, named Wallace, 'suddenly became enraged' and sprang at Macomo, pinning him against the side of the cage. Fortunately the animal was beaten off; Macomo was severely crushed and bitten, but still alive.

Ironically perhaps, when – some years later – death eventually did come to Macomo, it was a peaceful one; in bed, of fever, in the Palatine Hotel, Sunderland. Wallace was eventually destined for a very different fate.

Macomo was replaced as lion tamer by the singular presence and sight of Tom Macarthy. Yellowly was, it seems, fond of Macarthy: 'I knew him well; he was as brave as a lion, but rash and careless.' A possible indication of his previous carelessness was the fact that he only had one arm. His left arm had been torn off some years earlier during an incident with a lioness and Macarthy, undaunted, simply carried on with only his right. But, as Yellowly adds somewhat remorsefully, 'within a couple of years he was dead; killed while performing in a cage with five lions'.

So lion tamers came and went. The splendidly named Ledger Delmonico broke down his act, 'a most exciting performance', into imagined chronological episodes: 'The hunt, the fight, the capture and the reconciliation.' Awestruck audiences received demonstrations of his peerless hunting skills but also the subjugation of the will of these wild beasts to his own: 'The power man gains by firmness and kindness over the wild denizens of the forest.'

Of course, all this must have been very dramatic but perhaps the lion tamer with whom William Yellowly was most enamoured was a woman, a certain Mademoiselle Senide. She was, so he tells us, 'undoubtedly one of the most graceful and daring performers I have seen'. Like her fellow lion tamers, she was often seriously bitten and mauled, but she still showed a genuine love for her animals. Of 'fine presence and dignified bearing' she entered the arena, armed only with 'a light dog whip' and performed with two lions, an Indian panther and a Russian bear. The performance finished with 'the animals taking their places at a table, where she feeds them with raw flesh from her naked hand, while Augusta, the bear, regales himself with a pint of Bass's beer, which he drinks by holding the pot up to his mouth between his paws'.

However, Mademoiselle Senide would also be the victim of a curious and painful incident with a lioness and a photographer. To aid publicity for her act she decided to have herself photographed with her favourite lioness, Fatima. The artistic arrangement was agreed and the photograph was set up. For three minutes she waited whilst remaining rigidly in the pose agreed, as the photographer prepared, changed his mind, and then tinkered a bit more, before finally taking the exposure. Now, without doubt, three minutes is a long time to have your head in a lion's mouth, which was the position in which Mademoiselle Senide wished to be photographed. And Fatima, obligingly holding her mouth open for all that time, eventually 'got tired'. When the magnesium flash suddenly went off, finally taking the exposure, the dozing animal was startled and reacted instantly by snapping her jaws shut. The unfortunate Mademoiselle Senide received 'frightful wounds' to the neck and face, but refused to blame her beloved Fatima, putting full responsibility for the situation on the 'bungling' photographer.

Of course, it wasn't just the brave exploits of the lion tamers that thrilled the populace. Individual animals themselves, some with fierce reputations – deserved or not – drew in their own fans. Whether a giraffe or an American buffalo or bison, people flocked to see them. A great attraction was a notorious tiger, Nana Sahib, which had killed a jaguar and a full-grown lion. And people marvelled at a rhinoceros, advertised as 'The Unicorn of the Ancients', with a hide so thick and overlapping that 'it was said to be proof against a musket ball'. If only that were true in the twenty-first century!

William Yellowly was always keen to indulge his interest in taxidermy and, during the winter of 1861, Mrs Edmunds, a niece of George Wombwell, was at Sunderland with her collection. Yellowly visited the show, enquired as to whether there were any suitable deceased subjects, and 'brought away in a bag, an American skunk and a snake or two'.

Catching a train back home, he tells us that without another thought, he put the bag under his seat in the carriage. All did not go smoothly, however, as he reflects: 'Now a skunk, with its shining dark chocolate-brown coat and white bushy tail, is a very pretty and graceful animal to look at, but not to handle, even when dead.' A fact that very soon became apparent.

The day was cold and, as the carriage filled up with passengers, any open windows were securely closed to keep out the winter drafts. Soon after the train began to move; however, there was an alarming development as Yellowly himself relates: 'Whether it was from the handling and shaking while in the bag, or from the heat of the crowded compartment, I do not know; perhaps from both, but the train hardly got started when one of the most disgusting odours imaginable filled the compartment.'

At first everyone looked at each other politely but soon the overpowering 'fetid smell' became too much. Alarmed passengers were at a loss to explain it and began to discuss the possibilities, one man even suggested, rather curiously, that some matches must have taken fire as a reek of 'sulphurous gas combined with garlic, a hundred times concentrated' filled the compartment. The thoughts of the sheepish William Yellowly flew instantly to the decomposing contents of his bag and not a minute too soon the train arrived at South Shields. The grateful passengers hurried out into the cold but clear winter air and, as Yellowly tells us, 'taking up the bag, I made for home as quickly as possible'.

Apparently, after being left outside all through a cold night, the next morning the smell of decomposing skunk had subsided enough for Yellowly to be able to pursue his interest; an interest that immortalised not only the malodorous skunk, but also Wallace, the lion that had attacked Macomo. For the chronicles include a record which tells that after he died, Wallace 'was stuffed by William Yellowly of South Shields and is now (1888) in the Sunderland Museum'.

❧ ZOOLOGICAL CURIOSITIES ❧
(OR, A SHORT MISCELLANY OF NATURAL VISITATIONS)

Rare fish caught with a sausage!

So began an intriguing story which appeared on 8 September 2013 in the *Mail on Sunday*, of all places. The rare fish in question was a 3ft-long sturgeon, caught by two young boys using the aforementioned titbit as bait, during a fishing trip to Pembroke Dock, South Wales. No doubt the pair looked on askance when, after returning the fish to the water, they were told (perhaps in jest, but nevertheless in historical truth) that the sturgeon was a royal fish, and as such, should have been offered to Her Majesty.

Of course in centuries past, the king, or queen's law did not apply in the County Palatine of Durham, which instead followed the bishop's law. Any royal fish, therefore, actually become the bishop's. And it is recorded that in 1343, Bishop Bury laid claim to four such denizens of the deep, cast up on County Durham's shore; two whales and two sturgeons. The claim of the Prince Bishops of Durham to these prizes was taken very seriously and guarded very jealously. In 1387, Bishop Fordham directed his justices to take legal action against one Robert Browne of Hawthorne and three other offenders, for seizing and carrying away 'a certain porpoise, worth a hundred shillings', recently beached upon the shore. The bishop reiterated that 'all whales, sturgeons and porpoises, wrecked upon the coast of the Royal franchise of Durham by violence of the sea, were the undoubted right of himself and his predecessors'.

Indeed, the author remembers as a child seeing in some hidden recess of Durham's great cathedral, the skeleton of a whale, no doubt the royal prize of a distant prince bishop, and curiously out of place in such surroundings.

Interestingly, over the years, there have been repeated visits of such creatures. In 1662, Bishop John Cosin was offered five sturgeons by his steward at Howden, the bishop paying 6s 8d for each fish. They were duly brought to Durham, cooked, prepared and packed to be given as gifts to friends of the bishop. After being delivered of a subsequent bill for £5 17s 1d, the bishop was moved to point out that these charges were 'very considerable' and he took particular exception to some items: 'you need not have item'd me for your dill and rosemary!' Henceforward he instructed his steward at Howden 'to catch no more sturgeons'.

But such 'fish' continued to be seen over the centuries. A pod of whales was observed off South Shields in 1850. Eleven years previously, there was much excitement when an exotic-looking opah, or king fish, weighing in at 77lb and described by Sir Timothy Eden as 'a sort of gigantic, many hued mackerel', was caught off Hartlepool. And later a sturgeon, which would no doubt have terrified the two boys at Pembroke Dock, was landed near Stockton weighing 15 stone.

But it wasn't just maritime curiosities that were seen in Durham. St Nicholas' church, known familiarly as St Nic's, stands in Durham City's Market Place and predecessors of today's structure have stood on the same spot for centuries. An entry in the church register for the year 1568 records the following:

> The bringing to Durham of a very greate, strange and monstrous serpent, in length sixteen feet, in quantitie and dimensions greater than a greate horse, which was taken and killed by special pollicie in Etheopia, within the Turke's dominions; but before it was killed, it had devoured (as it is credibly thought) more than a thousand persons, and destroyed a whole countrey.

Thankfully, such a monstrous serpent as this was never seen alive in the County Palatine, apart of course from those legendary worms of Lambton and Sockburn, or perhaps as part of the sometimes bizarre collections of travelling menageries. However, it is reported that unfamiliar, strange and occasionally fearful creatures continued to be witnessed well into the nineteenth century.

There was, for example, consternation and no little fear across Victorian County Durham, when such a travelling menagerie 'caused quite a sensation', featuring, as one of its main attractions, a 'Wild Man'. Was it some kind of rare ape perhaps? Unknown, if not to science, then certainly to the good citizens of Spennymoor? Brought onto the stage in chains, for the purposes of entertainment, the unfortunate creature was goaded into picking up and brandishing an axe 'and displaying other characteristics of extreme savagery'. When a piece of red meat was thrown at it by the proprietor it began, 'to the intense horror of the spectators', to tear the raw flesh with its teeth. And so, for a few shows, over a few days, the citizens of Spennymoor packed in to see a spectacle that horrified and mesmerised them to the same degree.

Until that is, a small boy sneaked into the showground and peeped into the company's caravan to see the 'Wild Man', unchained, sitting round a table with the rest of the company, eating a cooked meal 'and speaking remarkably good English'. The mystery of the 'Wild Man' was solved and the spell was broken! Shortly afterwards, the show moved on.

Of course, in the mists of pre-history, real biological creatures, strange, curious and perhaps alarming, roamed the land that later became our county. We know this because of their skeletal remains. In the mid-twentieth century, the humerus of a woolly rhinoceros was unearthed near West Hartlepool. In 1939, the skeleton of a giant Irish elk was found at Neasham and two prehistoric ox skulls were dug out of Jarrow Slake. And in the remote crannies, crevices and caves of upper Weardale and Teesdale have been found the bones of long-dead wolves, wildcats, wild boar and lynx.

The historical record also gives instances of fleeting ornithological curiosities and of birds well out of their normal range and habitat. In 1909, mild sensation was aroused when a pure white starling was observed. In 1931 three avocets, uncommon wading birds, usually limited to the South Coast of England, were seen at Stockton. On 31 May of the same year, the song of a nightingale was heard near Rowland's Gill, which, as was stated, 'is well without the breeding area for this bird, which is, normally speaking, never heard north of York'. There were suspicions, though, that the bird in question had been a captive one which had been set free. Nonetheless, this was not the first time a nightingale had been heard in County Durham.

In the mid-1890s, its song had been heard at Windlestone and a Mr F. Burlinson recorded that people came 'from all arts and parts' to hear it; by bus, on horseback or on foot and 'in fact one could hear people walking the roads until the early hours of the morning'. There was even a poem written about it and published in the *Auckland Times and Herald* and Sir Timothy Eden, writing in the mid-twentieth century, reflected, rather lyrically, that 'there is something singularly moving in this picture of tired pitmen, pouring out in their hundreds in their char-a-banks, tramping the roads for hours, all to hear the voice of a nightingale, on a May night, long ago'.

But biological curiosities are not restricted to the long ago. In April 2012, a report appeared on the Internet describing how a giant rat had been killed in Consett, and in October the same year came reports of a seal observed in the River Wear, near Framwellgate Bridge, in the middle of Durham City. Some scoffed at the idea. The many witnesses must surely have been mistaken; it was perhaps an otter, known to frequent the river, though rarely, if ever, seen in daylight. Or perhaps, more prosaically, a rubber tyre, or a ball, bobbing along on the surface. After all, Durham City was far above the River Wear's tidal reaches and seals were not adapted for life in fresh water. Furthermore, by the time photographers from the local press arrived at the scene, 'the curiosity had disappeared'. Was there perhaps the faint aroma of hoax in the air?

So it was that in a state of some personal curiosity, the author himself went into Durham, expecting to see – well, nothing really! However, standing on Framwellgate Bridge and gazing downstream, a small group of wetsuited divers could be seen, busying about in the middle of the river, clearly taking part in one of their occasional visits to remove fallen tree debris from the water; their black, rubber-covered heads and backs, bobbing up and down in the water. Could this perhaps have been the origin of the sighting? Surely not!

A few days later, however, the truth was at last revealed when a photograph, published in the *Durham Times*, showed a seal in the River Wear at Chester-le-Street, chomping happily on a sizeable fish; perhaps the very same animal that had been seen a few miles upstream in Durham city. A spokesman for Durham Wildlife Trust later confirmed that it wasn't in fact that unusual for seals to occasionally venture so far upstream if they were following food, and of course at that time of year there occurs the autumn salmon and sea-trout run. So it seems that this wandering phocine phenomenon wasn't so unusual after all!

Perhaps the most evocative, ethereal encounter with a wanderer in the wilderness was experienced by Henry Tristram, Canon of Durham Cathedral, noted ornithologist and enthusiastic collector of over 10,000 avian specimens. One day, during the reign of Queen Victoria, he was alone, driving his horse over Stainmore, across the high, bleak moorland that separates County Durham from Cumbria. As often happens upon those heights, the weather took a turn for the worse, the clouds quickly closed in, and Canon Tristram suddenly found himself enveloped in thick fog. Unable to see his road ahead, he thought it unwise to proceed and pulled up his horse to wait for the fog to clear.

After a while there came the briefest of breaks in the weather and a thin ray of sunlight suddenly pierced the thick grey canopy and stretched its silver finger earthward, illuminating the very spot where the canon waited. A few seconds it seemed and it was snuffed out; the fog returned and once again gloom was all around. But in those few fleeting, glittering moments, a bright, brief instant in time, the good canon had seen a remarkable sight. For there, sitting motionless in the light, perched atop a boundary post only a few feet away from him and 'fixing him with its great yellow eyes, was an enormous golden eagle'. Canon Tristram waited excitedly for the fog to lift again, in the hope that the magnificent bird would still be there. But when the fog vanished, the eagle had vanished with it. The vision had gone!

⚜ ZURBARANS ⚜

Francisco de Zurbaran was a Spanish painter who worked during the time of the notorious Spanish Inquisition and specialised in religious themes and Biblical subjects.

Curiously, some of his works found their way from seventeenth-century Spain to Auckland Castle, now the official residence of the Bishop of Durham. Originally purchased under somewhat controversial circumstances, they have in recent years become somewhat controversial again.

The Zurbarans that now hang in Auckland Castle are thirteen monumental images, each 7ft high, representing the Biblical figure of Jacob, patriarch of the Jewish faith, and his twelve sons. As a collective work they depict chapter 49 of the Book of Genesis and represent the moment of Jacob's deathbed blessings to his sons; each of whom would become a progenitor of one of the twelve ancient tribes of Israel. Described as 'one of the most significant treasures of European Religious Art', it is thought that they were painted by Zurbaran as a symbolic statement, denouncing the religious intolerance of his day.

Their history and whereabouts before 1720 is not clearly known, though Zurbaran initially painted commissions for various religious establishments, so they may have been housed at some such place. Then there are vague stories; tales of the paintings being appropriated by pirates before finally coming into the possession of a Jewish Portuguese merchant, who in turn put them up for auction in 1756. And so it was that they were bought by Richard Trevor, Prince Bishop of Durham, but why?

In his book *County Durham*, written in the mid-twentieth century, Sir Timothy Eden acknowledged that Bishop Trevor had been responsible for buying 'eleven of those excellent and interesting Zurbaran's'. However he also, perhaps a little unfairly, described the bishop thus: 'He cannot be included in the small category of the great Bishops of Durham. He was extraordinary, neither as a thinker nor as a statesman, as a man of taste, however, he is not to be despised.'

In fact, in his day, Bishop Trevor had shown much sympathy with the Jewish community and growing social demands for multicultural acceptance, and had been instrumental in drafting legislation allowing Jews to become full British citizens. Parliament, however, had repealed the Bill and thus had angered and dismayed the bishop.

Subsequently, when the Zurbaran paintings became available, Bishop Trevor, conscious of their symbolic significance, seized the opportunity to purchase them and bring them back to Auckland Castle. He even had the Long Dining Room redesigned to house them. And so it would be that, at every official function, they would gaze down from the walls upon visiting statesmen and politicians. Their significance, 'to lament the failure of the lawmakers to grant freedom from oppression for the Jews in England', the bishop knew, would not be lost.

Curiously for 'a man of taste', but perhaps significantly, we are told that Bishop Trevor never bought another painting, of any kind, either before or after purchasing the Zurbarans.

So for over 250 years the paintings hung majestically in Auckland Castle, until, in 2009, doubts arose over their future and indeed over the future of Auckland Castle itself. Rumours began to circulate that the Church Commissioners were to sell the paintings, perhaps even the castle, in order to raise money for issues which they considered more pressing in twenty-first century Britain. Auckland

Auckland Palace around 1891.

Castle, for 800 years a residence of the Prince Bishops of Durham – probably even in use in the early eleventh century during the reign of King Cnut – and the precious Zurbaran paintings were in danger of being lost.

A high-profile public campaign was organised, involving Members of Parliament, the County Council and many local people. Grave concerns were raised about the future of what was considered a major part of County Durham's heritage. Eventually, through a very generous donation by a philanthropic businessman, both the castle and the paintings were 'saved for the people of the North East' and a charitable trust set up to protect their future.

It is still interesting to consider what Bishop Trevor originally paid for the works at auction, having not, it seems, 'bought' them, as Sir Timothy Eden tells us, 'from a Spanish pedlar'. Twelve of the thirteen paintings were purchased for £124, with individual prices ranging from £2 to £21. As one of the set was unavailable to purchase, the bishop paid another £21 for a copy of the final painting. From that seemingly relatively modest outlay in 1756, by 2009, it was thought that selling the Zurbarans of Auckland Castle would raise around £15 million.

Afterword

And so we close this book.

And if, as the writer sincerely hopes, the reader has enjoyed its content and wishes for more, then more there most certainly remains, for 'the seam to which reference has been made is by no means exhausted.'

We are indeed fortunate in the County of Durham in that, as the chronicles relate, 'no district in the British Isles is richer than our own in singular character or romantic interest'. And we are doubly fortunate that, as well as our great wealth of history and tradition, legends and stories, romances and biographical sketches, we have had in the past natives of our county with the interest and the foresight to record much of it, both for their own and for future generations.

Hopefully, in a modest way perhaps, this little book has 'restored to public use and enjoyment' at least some of the 'abundance of Antiquarian and other literature which has been accumulated and lain buried in forgotten histories'.

Such histories may well have been forgotten, but they are certainly not lost and anyone interested in exploring them further would be well advised to visit the Reference Library and request sight of those venerable volumes, of which a select few are listed in the bibliography; they may be assured that it would be well worth their while.

Bibliography

✛ STANDARD REFERENCES ✛

Billings, R.W., *Architectural Illustrations and Description of the Cathedral Church at Durham* (1843)

Fordyce, W., *The History and Antiquities of the County Palatine of Durham* (1855–1857)

Mackenzie, E. and Ross, M., *An Historical, Topographical and Descriptive View of the County of Durham* (1834)

Richardson, M.A., *Reprints of Rare Tracts* (1847–1849)

Richardson, M.A., *Stray Leaves of Northern History and Tradition* (1849)

Richardson, M.A., *The Local Historian's Table Book of Remarkable Occurrences* (1841–1846)

Surtees, R., *The History and Antiquities of the County Palatine of Durham* (1816–1823, 1840)

Sykes, J., *Local Records: Historical Register of Remarkable Events* (1824–1833)

The Monthly Chronicle of North-Country Lore and Legend (1887–1891)

The Victoria County History: A History of the County of Durham (1928 edition)

✛ FURTHER REFERENCES ✛

Ackroyd, Peter, *The English Ghost: Spectres through Time* (Chatto & Windus, 2010)

Alexander, M., *British Folklore, Myths and Legends* (2002)

Austin, John, 'Durham's Trout and Salmon Man' in *Durham Country* (winter, 1995)

Boyle, J.R., *The County of Durham* (1892)

Brockie, W., *Legends & Superstitions of the County of Durham* (1886)

Bygate, J.E., *The Cathedral Church of Durham: A Description of its Fabric and a Brief History of the Episcopal See* (London: George Bell & Sons, 1899)

Denham, M.A, *The Denham Tracts* (1846–1859)

Dodd, James, J., *The History of the Urban District of Spennymoor* (1897)

Eden, Sir Timothy, *County Durham* (1952)

Fawcett, J.W., *Tales of Derwentdale* (1902)

Gallop, A., *Buffalo Bill's British Wild West* (2001)

Heyes, William F. (compiler), *A Teesdale Bibliography* (Teesdale Record Society, 2009)

Hill, Frederick, *Local Stories of Fact, Fiction and Folklore* (Local Records of
    Washington, No. 3, 1944)
Hodgkin, J.E., *Durham* (1913)
Lake, Matt, *Weird England* (2007)
Low, J.L., *Diocesan Histories, Durham* (1881)
Matthews, S., *The Spectral Army of Souther Fell* (2011)
Mitton, G.E., *The County of Durham* (A&C Black & Co., 1924)
Ryder, Peter, *Finchale Priory* (English Heritage, 2000)
Mee, Arthur, *The King's England: Durham* (1953)
Westwood, J. and Simpson, J., *Haunted England* (Penguin Books, 2010)

⚜ WEBSITES ⚜

Specifically relating to the contents of this book:

BBC
British Hominid Research
Fortean Times
The Paranormal Database
The Zurbaran Trust

In addition to the above, there is a wealth of information available on the Internet.
Much of it makes interesting reading; however, care should be taken and it is for
the reader to satisfy themselves as to the veracity of individual websites.

Also from The History Press

EVER WONDERED WHAT YOUR TOWN USED TO LOOK LIKE?

Our *Then & Now* series sets out to illustrate the changing face of the UK's towns and cities in full colour. Contrasting a selection of forty-five archive photographs alongside forty-five modern photographs taken from the same location today, these unique books will compliment every local historian's bookshelf as well as making ideal gifts for everyone interested in knowing more about their hometown.

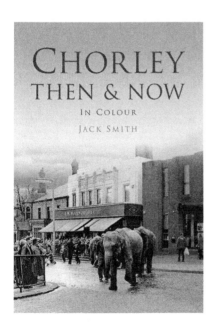

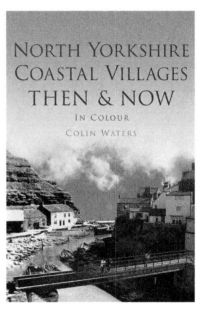

Find these titles and more at
www.thehistorypress.co.uk

Printed in Great Britain
by Amazon

73293995R00093